Astrologically Incorrect

Unlock the Secrets of the Signs to Get What You Want, When You Want!

Terry Marlowe

ADAMS MEDIA CORPORATION

Avon, Massachusetts

This book is for EYE,
with thanks for everything he is and does.

Published by
Adams Media Corporation
57 Littlefield Street, Avon MA 02322. U.S.A.
www.adamsmedia.com

ISBN: 1-58062-843-5

Printed in Canada.

J I H G F E D C B A

Library of Congress Cataloging-in-Publication Data
Marlowe, Terry.
Astrologically incorrect / by Terry Marlowe.
p.   cm.
ISBN 1-58062-843-5
1. Astrology. I. Title.
BF1708.1 .M374 2003
133.5–dc21

2002153894

This publication is designed to provide accurate and authoritative information with regard to the sub-ject matter covered. It is sold with the understanding that the publisher is not engaged in rendering legal, accounting, or other professional advice. If legal advice or other expert assistance is required, the services of a competent professional person should be sought.
—From a *Declaration of Principles* jointly adopted by a Committee of the
American Bar Association and a Committee of Publishers and Associations

Many of the designations used by manufacturers and sellers to distinguish their products are claimed as trademarks. Where those designations appear in this book and Adams Media was aware of a trademark claim, the designations have been printed with initial capital letters.

This book is available at quantity discounts for bulk purchases.
For information, call 1-800-872-5627.

Contents

Acknowledgments

I'd like to say a big thank you to my editor, Jill Alexander, who was wonderful to work with throughout the process. Thanks also to Paul Beatrice, Laura MacLaughlin, and Khrysti Nazzaro. Many thanks to my agents, Sheree Bykofsky Associates, especially Sheree Bykofsky and Janet Rosen. Hi, guys.

Also, thanks to those who read the manuscript in its various incarnations: Gail Fortune, Diane Sullivan, and Marcia Talley. Very special thanks to Deborah Crombie for offering her suggestions and being supportive above and beyond the call of friendship.

Thanks are also due to Carol Chase, Frank Cody, Shirley Crow, Stuart Crow, Bob Boehler, Peter Sanford, Walter Satterthwait, Toby Threadgill, and my family: Janet, Craig, Jerry, and Geneva.

Lastly, I owe a debt of gratitude to Ira "Eye" Lipson, for his guidance and encouragement.

Foreword

Yes, things are slow at work. But your Aries boss isn't. Yesterday, Aries asked you to put together a quick feasibility study about the restaurant she's opening. All you have to find out is the cost of the equipment, whether you can use the old plumbing, and if you really have to get the Department of Health involved if you serve food.

Just as you've made a list of people to call, your boss says, "Where are they?"

You: Where are what?
Aries Boss: The numbers.
You: (stammering) But you only gave me . . . but it was only yesterday. I don't know yet.
Aries Boss: And you wanted a raise? Forget it.

Suddenly you remember, you should act instantly when an Aries boss gives orders.

You've just gotten home and what you discover sends you into a panic. Dinner guests will arrive in thirty minutes and there's no food in the house.

Your considerate yet elusive Pisces lover should've done the shopping yesterday, but he didn't. And he isn't home yet. And every time you call his office, you get sent to voice-mail purgatory.

v

Just as you're about to toss the phone into the toilet, your Pisces lover enters.

You:	Where were you?
Pisces Lover:	At work. What's wrong with you?
You:	You weren't at work—I know because I called. Where the hell were you? And what about dinner?
Pisces Lover:	What about it?

Then he leaves. You fume as the door slams. Then you see you were right: Pisces wasn't at work this afternoon. Pisces was out shopping instead and left a bag filled with wine and appetizers just inside the door to prove it.

Suddenly, you remember if you check up on a Pisces lover, he'll vanish.

The repo man from American Express keeps calling. You can't figure out where all these mysterious charges are coming from. You've never had tea in London. You've never sipped café au lait in Paris. But you did have a few laughs and cocktails with your Sagittarius best friend the week before and heard all about her upcoming trip to Europe.

You recall that right before closing time, you said, "Sure, use my credit card," then went to the restroom. You meant Sagittarius should clear the bar tab. Sagittarius misunderstood.

Then you remember Sagittarius is literal-minded—and has an imperfect understanding of credit card limits.

It looks as though you forgot whom you were dealing with. More important, you forgot how to deal with them. Do you want to learn how to manage the different astrological signs? Go even further: Find out how to manipulate them instead.

Introduction:
The Case for Craftiness

It's easy to find books on how to take charge of your own life. But where do you find advice on how to take charge of *other* people's lives? Astrology's here to help.

Everyone's heard of sun signs—that's the sign under which you were born. It's what people are referring to when they say, "I'm a Libra" or "I'm a Scorpio." Sun signs are an important part of your horoscope. But they are not the only part. Only a complete horoscope will give a psychological profile and expose every one of an individual's fetishes, neuroses, and hang-ups.

Usually it's not possible to get the information you need to run a full astrological chart. Also, unless you're an astrologer, you wouldn't know how to read it anyway. Even if you could, what's it got to do with compelling your boss to give you a raise, getting your spouse to screw the cap on the toothpaste, or enticing your lover to submit to your sultry charms? You've tried the direct approach. You've tried one-on-one, sensitive New Age conversations.

Now try manipulation.

The Rising Sign and the Sun Sign

Pretend you're blackmailing your neighbor for $20,000. Would you expect to get paid if you didn't know his secrets? Of course not! Then why do you think you can manage someone in even the most mundane matter if you don't know how his or her mind works?

Manipulation virgins fail because they don't know enough about their targets. The artful strategist dissects her subject's personality to expose his vulnerable spots. Some practitioners rely on psychology. Or intuition. But astrology is the easiest way to find out how another person's mind works—and how to get it to work in your best interest.

Of all the parts of a horoscope, the sun sign and rising sign are the most revealing and the easiest to figure out. Imagine that each part of your horoscope represents a different kind of party. The sun sign is a "come as you are" party. The rising sign's a "come as you *wish* you were" party.

Just as the sun is the center of the solar system, the sun sign is the center of your personality. It tells what makes you tick. The rising sign is also an integral part of any horoscope and a key to understanding yourself and others. The rising sign is your personality and your self-protective public mask. It's what you hide behind; the behavioral rabbit you pull out of the hat when you're cornered. The rising sign is what you appear to be and what you think you ought to be.

In a society that's determined to plumb the depths of superficiality, the compulsion to live up to our "image" is overwhelming. And while we're preening in the rearview mirror, we're just asking to get rear-ended.

When you want to handle someone in a cunning way, look up both the sun sign and the rising sign. The combination will tell you everything you need to know about the person—and the best way to get what you want.

If you're like most people, you'll check out your own sun and rising signs first, just to test the techniques before using them on someone else. (Or to protect yourself from being manipulated.) You may think the description doesn't fit, and that astrology's a bunch of crap. But ask your boss to read it. Or your best friend. Then watch them collapse with laughter at how well it fits you. Let's face it: Unless you're very introspective or have spent lots of cash on therapy, you won't acknowledge your weak spots. After all, if you knew what manipulated you, you wouldn't be manipulated by it.

As you look up a person's sun and rising signs, remember one or the other will be more obvious to certain people at certain times or in particular situations. For instance, a Capricorn rising steadily climbs his way into influence and the Social Register. But if he has an Aries sun, he'll piss off a lot of people on the way.

Or maybe your coworkers rely on your practical, budget-conscious Taurus rising qualities at the office. But your family knows there's a Pisces sun underneath who takes in strays and spends all her weekly paycheck on hallucinogens in the first three days.

If these traits sound contradictory, they are. People are. It's why retrograde hippies say, "Hey, live and let live," and why the rest of us, who live in the real world, get to play dirty.

Here's how.

2

How to Get the Most from This Book: Using the Sun Sign and the Rising Sign to Dance the Astrological Tactics Tango

Successful manipulation is a tactical dance. It means protecting your flank, pulling your own strings, and pushing other people's buttons. Discover your own powers and vulnerabilities as described by the sun and rising signs. Learn the strengths and weaknesses of your partner in the manipulation dance. Then use your knowledge to protect yourself while taking advantage of the other person.

The first part of this chapter gives an overview of how to get what you want from others by using knowledge of their sun and rising signs. The second part tells you how to calculate the rising sign and ends with a list of sun sign dates.

The rest of the book devotes a chapter to each of the twelve astrological signs. Every chapter hands you the ammunition you need to take charge of each sign as well as to devise innovative strategies of your own.

How to Find the Sun Sign and Use It

First, start with the sun sign. Look up your own at the end of this chapter. Then look up the sun sign of somebody you'd like to handle in a cunning way. All you need to know is a birth date.

For example, let's say there's friction in your love life. You look up your sun sign and find out you're a Virgo. Then you look up your lover's sun sign and discover he's an Aquarius. You don't want to be picky, but your avant-garde Aquarius lover won't do the dishes. You've lectured and lectured, but each time it gets worse instead of better. Now what?

Read Chapter 8 on Virgo. This reminds you that you're intelligent, that you like order and schedules, and that you have the kind of loving relationship with your day-planner that other people have with their pets.

Then you read Chapter 13 and realize you're living with a rebellious Aquarius, whose idea of hell is hearing the buzz of an alarm clock and having to do anything or be anywhere on someone else's schedule.

Your penchant for routine and propensity for lecturing clashes with your Aquarian lover's disdain for schedules and authority figures. You tried the direct approach and it didn't work. Now be cagey.

Play on Aquarius's need to be cutting-edge and different. Housework is ordinary, so you'll have to hide its bourgeois nature by making it seem radical to Aquarius. For example, put a CD player in the kitchen and surround it with trendy alternative-music CDs. Then do the dishes yourself a few times: at three o'clock in the morning. Aquarius may not say anything, but he'll notice. You'll wake up one day, and the sink will not only be empty but gleaming. Who cares what time he did the dishes? They're done.

How to Use the Sun Sign and the Rising Sign

You came out on top in that skirmish with your lover just by knowing about sun signs. Now refine your knowledge and twist it to your tactical advantage by using the rising sign as extra leverage. This time, let's use a different sun sign and another situation as an example.

Maybe you have problems with a friend who volunteered to house-sit while you were out of town. After a long week's business trip, you came home to find piled-up newspapers and dried-up houseplants. What should you do? Before doing anything, look up your rising sign. You can find it on the Web at *www.terrymarlowe.com* under "Rising Sign Tables," or by doing an Internet search for astrological rising sign tables. If you don't have access to the Internet, befriend a computer geek or consult your local library.

Let's say you're a Sagittarius sun sign with Cancer rising. Read Chapter 11 first, where you'll learn that you're more at home in a hotel room than your own house and that you're open and forthright with people.

But you also have Cancer rising. Chapter 6 reminds you of how much you love your home and that you approach people and issues indirectly. You suspect there's a contradiction here. Which are you: Sagittarian or Cancerian?

You're both.

Mix the two signs and it means you can turn a hotel room into a cozy home, and you always carry prepaid phone cards so you can call home while you're on the road. When you tackle issues and people, you may start indirectly. But once you know what you want to address, you're frank to the point of bluntness.

Now that you're aware of how you operate, think of how other people deal with you. Your friends, for example. Sometimes they'll play on the Cancerian indirectness when it suits them, especially when there's an issue they want you to avoid, like the fact they forgot to water your houseplants while you were out of town.

Now, the houseplant assassin knows your Sagittarian side wants to tell her off with some accurate but painful truths. So she pushes the Cancer button by saying something like, "I sure missed your advice on how to rearrange furniture."

Normally, you would've made suggestions about armchairs and armoires. Now you know better and don't react the way your friend expects.

Gain insight into your friend by using the same methods you used to learn about yourself. For instance, you want to know how to handle the houseplant incident. Look up your friend's sun sign and rising sign to find out the best way to manipulate her.

Let's say your friend has a Gemini sun sign. This means she's curious, verbal, easily distracted, and was on her way to water your plants when something more interesting came along and made her forget your address. Your Gemini friend also has Pisces rising, which tells you she's sympathetic, intuitive, and not confrontational.

Here's how to confront the situation: You've returned from the airport to find your geraniums have withered and the climbing ivy has stopped climbing. You know that your friend's Gemini side likes to talk and loses conversational direction as easily as her geographical bearings. So, play on it. Chat about your trip. Use the opportunity to lead the conversation around to your point. This will divert your friend's Gemini side from her Pisces rising side, which senses you're about to say something hurtful: like the truth.

You could say something like, "Yes, it was a great trip. It's too bad my plants wilted while I was gone."

Now you've jerked the sympathetic Pisces chain and pushed the

Gemini sun behind a cloud. Your friend's Pisces side is aghast at the state of your plants. And she will probably buy you new ones.

By learning about yourself and your friend through astrology, you've used your strengths to play on your friend's weaknesses. You've danced the tactics tango. And you've gotten what you wanted.

 Other Sun Sign and Rising Sign Combinations
We examined how to combine a Cancer sun sign or rising sign with a Sagittarius sun sign or Sagittarius rising, and a Gemini sun sign or rising sign with a Pisces sun sign or Pisces rising. Chapter 15 has examples of how other astrological signs affect each other.

How to Calculate the Rising Sign

It's easier to find the rising sign than you may think. First, you need to know the day and month of your potential victim's birthday. And where he was born. Narrowing it down to a time zone is enough.

The next part is trickier. You have to find out what time he was born. Or at least within a couple of hours, because that's how often the rising sign changes to a new sign.

A birth time shouldn't be too hard to find if we're talking about a family member. Birth certificates usually have birth times. If not, family reminiscences can provide the information, for example: "Grandmother said the sun was just going down about the time your mother was born."

Or maybe you'd like to manipulate your boss. You can usually find out a birthday with no problem. But to find out your boss's birth time, you'll need to dig deeper in a subtle way. Try the following at the next office happy hour.

You: *(to your boss)* You're always so bright and on top of things every morning.

Boss: I've always been a morning person.

You: That's obvious by how you take charge first thing. I've noticed a lot of people who were born at night are nightowls, and people born during the day are morning people. I know it's true with me; my brain doesn't kick in until lunchtime.

Now your boss is hooked. Early risers can be notoriously self-righteous.

Boss: You're right. I was born at six-thirty in the morning, and I love getting up with the sun.

Now you have a birth time. And you've also had a little up-front practice at manipulating.

If the Birth Time's Not Exact

You've gotten your subject's birthday and an approximate time of birth. Then you look up the time in the rising sign tables on the Web, and you find the time is on the border between two signs. Luckily, it's easy to tell where a person's personality falls because of the way the signs follow each other around the zodiac. Each sign is very different from the one next to it.

For example, a Leo rising will dominate a room; a Virgo rising will try to clean it. Read the chapters for both astrological signs, and it'll be obvious which rising sign fits.

If it's impossible to get a person's birth time, you can still find his or her vulnerable spots. Just use the sun sign alone.

As you work your way through this book and dabble in premeditated manipulation, you might feel guilty at first. Then you'll probably feel a mischievous sense of power.

Revel in it.

Sun Sign Dates

Aries: March 20–April 20

Taurus: April 21–May 21

Gemini: May 22–June 21

Cancer: June 22–July 23

Leo: July 24–August 23

Virgo: August 24–September 23

Libra: September 24–October 23

Scorpio: October 24–November 22

Sagittarius: November 23–December 21

Capricorn: December 22–January 20

Aquarius: January 21–February 19

Pisces: February 20–March 19

Note: Sun sign dates are approximate. The exact dates shift around by a day or so, depending on the year.

3

Aries, the Ram:
Trolling for Trauma

Looking for an Equal: I'm holding a contest and if you reach me first, you win. Don't waste my time if you're less than tasty, intelligent, athletic, daring, and can take the occasional conversational hit. Call me. Now.

Aries sun:	March 20–April 20
Planetary ruler:	Mars
Aries Web site:	*www.runs/wth/scissors*

Aries is the sign of action, which means you'll get nowhere fast if you don't move faster. It's a rarely discussed but well-known fact that you can't manipulate someone if you can't catch the person. And you're apt to catch the Ram doing just about anything, because fear is as foreign to Aries as sincerity is to a used-car salesperson.

Aries is the first sign of the zodiac, so the solar system revolves around Arians. Or so they assume. The price of admission to the Ram's universe is to become a whizzing little planet, so pretend you're orbiting and manipulate your Aries instead.

Dealing with the Doyenne of Domination

Aries' planetary ruler is Mars, the god of war. This means the sign is basically a dominant one. To manipulate the sign successfully, maintain the illusion that Aries is in charge. If you're dealing with an Aries lover, friend, or boss, follow these rules while pretending to submit.

Be Direct

Aries is literal-minded. If you drop hints, Aries won't get them. They'll merely clutter up the floor, which slows down Aries' forward motion. That pisses him off.

→ *Lesson:* Don't drop hints.

Get to the Point

When talking to Aries, keep to the point and have a point to keep to. By all means, share your deep insights. But don't go too deep. Your version of covert complexity is the Ram's idea of overt whining.

→ *Lesson:* By the time you finish your convoluted sentence, the Ram has finished her conversation with you.

Obey Orders

Or pretend to. Giving orders is Aries' job. Obeying them is yours. Aries often forgets you're a competent adult and tells you things you already know. Attempting to tell her that you remember how to get to the post office, that you know where the dog's leash is kept, and that you've ridden in a car before is a waste of your breath and Aries' time.

➻ *Lesson:* Don't expect submissiveness.

Respond to Aries—Immediately

Don't keep Aries waiting. Aries may be the master of his fate and the captain of everyone else's soul, but he hasn't mastered the skill of patience. In fact, the genetic ability to wait is missing from the Mars-ruled Ram's DNA strand. He has no interest in cultivating patience and considers it a waste of time.

➻ *Lesson:* If you keep Aries waiting, you'll wait forever—for him to come back.

Recognizing Aries

Aries has attributes the other astrological signs lack, so recognizing her takes very little perception and no aim. Aries' unique mixture of traits is quite charming and delightful to be around. Twist them to your advantage.

Idealism. Aries is the idealist of the zodiac. The ideal world is one in which Aries swashbuckles his way through hardships, car-chase scenes, and romantic encounters. This is the world in which Aries lives. Hit him with real-world reality and he'll fold like a cheap suit.

Impetuousness. The Ram's bravery often leads her to react without considering the consequences. For most of us, challenges trigger certain primal programming: Stimulus→Thought→Reaction. With Aries, the process is different: Stimulus→Action. Notice that the "thought" segment is missing. This is your chance to steer Aries into taking the action you want her to take.

Absence of modesty. Aries is willing to admit he's not only the first but also the kindest, most intelligent, not to mention best-looking sign of the zodiac. All Rams agree; and since you can't beat them, join them.

Sartorial elegance. To make sure you notice her, sometimes Aries will try on a small ego. It doesn't fit.

Are you in the mood to manipulate Aries? This is hazardous, because the Ram is against manipulation. It enrages his sense of idealism.

Aries is aboveboard and expects you to be the same. Mix this with the well-known Ram penchant for solving problems in a truthful, impetuous, and martial way, and you'll see that learning how to move fast is essential to your safety.

→ *Lesson:* If you manipulate Aries and get caught, the Ram will shoot now and worry about how he'll look on probation later. But chances are, Aries won't catch you. Fortunately for manipulative purposes, the sign is skimpy on introspection and a stranger to subtlety.

 The Aries Achilles' Heel: A Challenge
Aries knows a thrown-down gauntlet when she sees one. A challenge is the one thing Aries can't resist.

The Fundamental Rule of Manipulation

Since Aries is infatuated with competition, you'll often find him in contests. It could be a contest over who drives the fastest, who gains access to the executive suite first, or who can drain a bank account with the most panache. Whatever the contest, in whatever type of relationship you have with Aries, remember this fundamental rule: Never let Aries win.

Imagine you're playing a game. It could be a game like Monopoly or marriage. You think the best way to please your competitive Aries is to give her what she wants: victory.

The stakes are high and it's your turn. You own Park Place and Boardwalk. Aries is one throw of the dice away from landing on either, but she doesn't have the rent money and can't mortgage her railroads again.

> Aries: If you buy a hotel for Boardwalk and I land on it, you'll win. (Aries always gives instructions, even when it's not in her best interests.)
> You: Maybe next turn.

Aries scowls, so naturally you think she's happy. When it's your turn again, you roll the dice, land on Aries' railroad, can't pay the rail fare, and lose the game. Now you assume the Ram's really happy. You're wrong.

➥ *Lesson:* Aries only likes the person who beats her. If you let Aries win, it'll be the last contest you'll ever have.

Yes, the relationship is an eternal contest. Yes, it's wearing and leads to Aries' irritability. But this is a natural Aries state. It's better to be inflicted with an irritated Ram than with a bored one. When Aries is bored, she'll go find someone else who'll flog back.

Challenging Aries to Do It Your Way

Play on Aries' competitiveness when you'd like the Ram to do something unpleasant or tedious. Here are a few ways to get him right where you want him.

Use Compliments

Perhaps you'd like Aries to rewire your stereo system. You could always just ask. But Aries could always just say no. And once Aries refuses, he rarely reconsiders.

> You: We could listen to music, but my stereo's broken. It's too bad. You have great taste in music and a wicked way with a sound system.
> Aries: Where's your electrical outlet?
>
> ➻ *Lesson:* Pay Aries a compliment. It's no more than he expects, and it will get you what you deserve.

Try Insults

Dare to say you can do something better than Aries. Any time you loot her confidence, she considers it an insult. And a challenge.

Suppose you want Aries to do a little motor maintenance. Aries would rather do something dashing, like go bike racing. To encourage the Ram to open a tool kit instead of inflate bike tires, try this:

> You: I'm sure you could replace that battery perfectly well. But I can probably do it faster.
> Aries: Right. Watch me.
>
> ➻ *Lesson:* Get Aries to do anything you want by playing on her competitiveness.

Encourage Action

➻ *Lesson:* Don't ask yes or no questions. If you do, the reflex answer will be: "No!" Instead, phrase a request in a way that demands action as the answer.

> You: We've got two options. We can sit here and wait to be arrested. Or we can put our clothes on and drive to my house.
> Aries: Don't tell me what to do. We'll drive to your house.

Exactly what you wanted him to do in the first place.

Traipsing the Tightrope: The Aries Lover

The Aries lover is a relationship kamikaze. Not only does he rush in where angels fear to tread but enjoys a romantic fight to the death. And if you're not having one, he'll stir one up. Keep that in mind so you'll remember how potentially terminal this encounter really is.

An Aries lover is infuriatingly contradictory. Not only does the Ram contradict other people, but himself, too. This makes a love relationship hard to manage. Mainly because of the difference between what Aries wants and what Aries thinks he wants.

On one hand, Aries wants you to kneel and kiss the hem of his garment. If you do, he wants you to get off your knees and get a life. On the other hand, Aries expects you to be worldly, chic, and experienced. If you are or act like you are, he'd rather you be a social, sexual, and political virgin.

Attracting Aries is the easy part. Now that you've intrigued him, Aries holds an internal contest between idealism and the need to conquer. Idealism loses. The Ram will make the first move—probably before you cross his line of vision. Forget formal introductions and long courtships.

By tweaking his interest, you've opened a window of opportunity. If you jump in too fast, Aries will think you're not worth getting. Wait too long, and he'll forget your phone number and hair color. Still, it helps to set yourself apart from the crowd. Try the following to pique Aries' romantic interest.

Aries Turn-Ons

Be reckless. Aries has a true taste for risk.

➺ *Lesson:* Be impetuous. Aries knows what it's like to jump first and think shortly before death. Take up motorcycling, car racing, hot-air ballooning, or any endeavor that's showily scintillating and potentially fatal.

Show off. Parade your charms, wits, and assets. Aries likes dash, flash, panache. If all you have to show for yourself is modesty, the Ram will trip over you while heading for the nearest Marilyn Monroe look-alike. If he does notice you, he'll delegate you to the nearest Pisces or Virgo, to whom modesty is considered sexy.

➡ *Lesson:* Aries wants somebody who's good enough–for Aries.

Keeping the Aries Lover Interested

There are two distinct phases in the Aries love relationship: attracting and maintaining. Same person. Different game.

To attract a Ram is easy. To keep Aries around is a test of stamina, recklessness, and endurance. It's a balancing act between "I want to run off with you to the south of France," and "What did you say your name was?" Try this:

Keep your distance. Don't give in at the first approach. Remember Aries' appetite for challenge. This is especially true in love.

➡ *Lesson:* Once Aries has conquered you–or thinks she has– she'll lose interest. Instantly. But not necessarily permanently.

Beat a strategic retreat. Aries has propositioned you. But you'd like to spend some vertical time together first, so try this:

> You *(whispering seductively)*: If we do this now, I'd have
> nothing to look forward to.
> Aries: Good point.

➡ *Lesson:* Show interest but don't give in.

By stepping back, you've pushed the challenge button. And twitched the tightrope. Now Aries will pursue you.

How to Keep the Aries Lover from Bolting

Now that Aries has pursued you into romantic submission and you're in an actual relationship, you have challenges of your own. In the long term, there are a couple of problems with Aries lovers.

Problem 1. Aries will stay enamored for as long as you're readily available but just out of reach, attentive yet not smothering, devoted yet independent, perfect yet attainable. And faultless.

Problem 2. Aries will be monogamous for as long as you live up to his ideals. Since Aries ideals are impossible to live up to, you see the problem. Cope with these difficulties by preventing romantic boredom. To keep Aries interested and yourself off lithium, try the following techniques:

- *Argue for sport.* Aries calls this "entertaining and energetic conversation." Everyone else calls it unnecessary wear and tear on the argument sector of your cerebral cortex.
- *Take charge of the finances.* Being an idea person, the Ram has the idea that money should be circulated. While this theory is economically sound in a recession, in practice it can be embarrassing.

> You: I'm sure you remembered to run to the post office and mail the utility bills.
>
> Aries: Forget the utilities. You've always wanted a piano, right? Look what I picked up on the way home.

Yes, you'd like to see its beauty. You know you own a beautiful new grand piano, but you can't admire it because you have no electric light.

➥ *Lesson:* The Aries approach to money is sound economics. To the bank, it's financial promiscuity.

- *Handle paperwork.* Aries would rather you handle details like ordering new checkbooks, filling out loan applications, and renewing magazine subscriptions. But she'll put up a token fight if you volunteer. Try this:

You: Let me sort out the paperwork this month. You need time off to think of more important things.

Aries: Well, okay.

Aries Lover Don'ts

Don't fool around. Be faithful. Recall the Aries idealism. Remember the tirades. Ideal loves don't screw around.

Don't be jealous. Aries can be jealous. But you can't. Aries will say how jealous she isn't while scrolling through your caller-ID for unidentified phone numbers of possible rivals. Aries doesn't like it when you notice other people. Because it means you're not noticing her.

Say you've been to a party and Aries fumed the whole trip home.

You: *(to your Aries wife)* Why are you so pissed off that I sat next to your sister at the dinner party?

Aries: You talked to her the whole evening.

You: What about the night you had dinner with your old boyfriend and dragged in at two in the morning?

Aries: That's different.

➻ *Lesson:* When it comes to jealousy, it's a one-way street. Resist the temptation to leave your dictionary open to the page that defines hypocrisy.

Don't bore Aries. To sustain your relationship and mental equilibrium, keep Aries from getting bored. The best way to do it is to disappear. Aries is frantic. What happened? Where are you?

Just come back. Don't explain. Aries will start over. You've become the Aries ideal: readily available but just out of reach, attentive yet not smothering, devoted yet independent, perfect yet attainable. Now you're irresistible.

Again.

The Aries Boss

An Aries boss is easier to deal with than an Aries lover. You expect to obey a boss.

The business world would be a dull place without Aries. She's an innovator. A pioneer. The wizard of brainstorming. If it weren't for Aries, our culture would be devoid of things such as sales seminars and push advertising.

Your Aries boss is an idea person. She has so many brilliant ideas she's bound to forget some of them. Pray that she does, because you can't execute all of them and still have time to take lunch or even a deep breath.

Part of your job is to cull through the brilliant ideas, decide which are practical as well as inspired, and then set them in motion.

Here's how to take full advantage of the Aries boss.

Take Action Immediately

Make a phone call. Send an e-mail. Write a letter. Prove you're doing something. Then secretly cull through the list of Aries' ideas and present your narrowed-down list.

You: Here are your ideas.
Aries: Brilliant job.

Use Your Time Wisely

You've spent a long time on a project for your Aries boss. He's bound to be pleased with your work. You present your carefully researched findings.

Aries: Why the hell did you waste six months studying useless productivity targets?

You: (*sotto voce*) Because you told me to.

Aries: Quit mumbling. That was just an idea for a quick project. Can't you figure these things out for yourself? I've known what to do since the age of three.

➡ *Lesson:* An Aries boss would rather get something quickly than have it submitted perfectly.

Communicate Directly

Go directly to Aries when you have a problem, even if she is three rungs above you on the corporate ladder. Wading through intermediaries wastes time. Once you've chased down Aries, cut to it or she'll chase you from the office.

Talk fast, too. There's nothing convoluted about Aries' communication style. This is refreshing, because it reduces the chances of miscommunication. It's also painful, because Aries lops off conversational leads and rarely comes equipped with tourniquets.

➡ *Lesson:* Follow your boss's communication lead and respond by saying things like:

- "Let's go."
- "Now."
- "Do it."
- "Done."

Strike Back

An Aries boss respects strength, especially in employees. Stand up to him. Talk back.

→ *Lesson:* Be impertinent with your Aries boss. It pays.

Your Aries boss is fuzzy on the concepts of cash flow, the gold standard, and the time value of money. After spending twenty minutes trying to explain, you finally lose patience and ask if he's ever seen a positive balance on an income statement.

Then Aries smiles and treats you to something you'd never have heard if you hadn't challenged him: "Lunch. Let's go."

♈ ♈ ♈

When manipulating dynamic Aries, remember he has an abundance of charming traits, but modesty's not one of them. So it's not surprising that a conversation with Aries is a conversation about Aries. This knowledge of Aries' favorite subject comes in handy when you try to get your way. Also be aware of the Aries penchant for crisis management, which prods the Ram into swashbuckling through six disasters before breakfast. If you don't plot carefully, your attempt to manipulate this sign could be one of those disasters. Careless maneuvering around Aries can be like checking for gas leaks with a lighted match. Try it if—like Aries—you feel reckless and unafraid. After all, you've got to admire the Aries courage—it's mandatory.

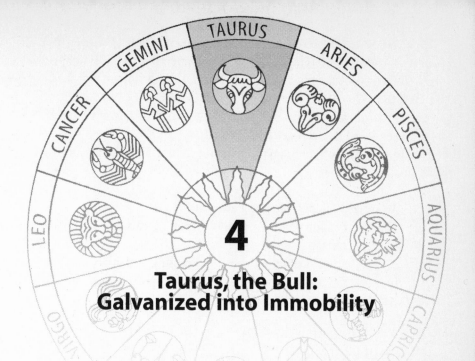

4

Taurus, the Bull: Galvanized into Immobility

I'm thrifty and reliable. So you don't need to be. I'm not interested in world travel. But I am interested in traveling back in time to the days when television was broadcast in black and white and music was played in mono. Our time machine must be equipped with culinary comforts and enable me to leap across the time/space continuum without rising from my comfortable chair.

Taurus sun:	April 21–May 21
Planetary ruler:	Venus
Taurus Web site:	*www.root-bound*

Have you run into constant and single-minded Taurus? You'll know it when you do. The Bull is solid—impenetrable, even. He has no armor you can chink, no rungs you can climb, and no peripheral vision that I know of. This tunnel vision is how you can take advantage of Taurus. Unless you plot something within his line of vision, he won't see it. So you can get away with it.

Taurus can be found anyplace he can flaunt his solidity and traditionalism, such as:

- An office building, plugging away at his job
- The Rotary Club or Junior League, listening patiently to the featured speaker
- A bank, either making a deposit or refusing a loan application
- In a car, fantasizing about exceeding the speed limit so he can get home as soon as possible

Beware of Obstacles

Beneath Taurus's easy-going and laid-back facade lies a formidable opponent. Taurus doesn't take action because she doesn't need to. Her defense system and bull-like solidity are all she needs to protect herself from little pishers who try to manipulate her. Whether your Bull is a friend, lover, or employer, read on to find out the obstacles you must bore your way through.

The Barricade of Pragmatism

When you want something from Taurus, ask yourself: Is it practical? If it isn't, make it seem so. Far-flung and fanciful schemes are as foreign to the Bull as compassion is to an IRS auditor. Present a practical, realistic plan. For something to be real, Taurus must be able to see it, touch it, eat it, or deposit it in a high-yield mutual fund.

For example, you want to convince your Taurus husband to put a fountain in the backyard. You need to:

- Have a plan
- Present it in a concrete way
- Approach Taurus in plenty of time

Specifically, approach Taurus in the autumn to be ready for construction in the spring. Have the plans drawn up, estimate the cost and how you'll pay for it, and show him the architect's full-color elevations. Then give him time to think about it.

➻ *Lesson:* Plan ahead, and don't push for an answer.

The Detour

This is yours because Taurus takes no detours or side trips. Taurus is like a fanatic driver who targets her vacation destination and won't stop for anything frivolous (like bathroom breaks or food and water). On the road of life, Taurus won't change plans once she gets going, so you'd better figure out a creative way to reach your goals without trying to get your Bull to change hers.

➻ *Lesson:* Learn to sidestep Taurus when she's entrenched—which is always.

The Wall of Single-Mindedness

Taurus's tunnel vision means he won't notice what you're up to when you're manipulating him. So just carry on with your plotting and planning. Chances are, he won't catch you. And even if he does, you won't hear about it until your mission is accomplished.

The Practical Bull

The astrologically uninitiated say that Bulls are boring. They're not. They're just predictable. This can be comforting, especially if you've been flitting around with a wild Aquarius or a calendar-deprived Gemini. Taurus tantalizes you with the sensation of safety. Bulls are the agents provocateurs for a stable life. It can be very seductive. Just look at Taurus: She's so well adjusted. It just shows what years of clean living will do to a person.

Taurus's Achilles' Heel: Losing Security

Taureans fear losing security, either physical or emotional. According to astrological wisdom, cash represents security to a Taurus. This can be just a symbol, though. Taurus can define security in any number of ways: a home, a car, a corner office, a school, or a wardrobe. It could also be you. Whatever it is, be warned that Taurus will hold onto it with a possessiveness that would even put Cancer to shame. So tread carefully.

All this down-to-earth practicality means that Bulls rarely experience feelings of paranoia. It's not that they're obtuse. Quite the contrary! They simply have no radar for anything that deviates from a straight and narrow, preplanned path or agenda. This gives you the opportunity to be manipulative. What fun! To manipulate them successfully, you must stand in their path and seem to play on their terms. It helps to put on a front. Here are a couple of guises you should adopt.

SEEM TO BE	ACTUALLY ARE
Stable	Underhanded
Straightforward	Crafty (Then go over his/her head.)

Try the following manipulation meditation: Visualize leading Taurus down the garden path, through a door and into a fragrant room with plush draperies, furnishings, and floor coverings. Then pull the rug out from under him. This is the best way to catch Taurus off-guard.

Digging into the Taurus Stereotypes

There are a couple of stereotypes that are unworthy of comment. It's an exaggeration to say all Bulls are maniacally miserly. They just like the accumulation, of material assets, and what's wrong with that?

It's untrue that the only time that Taurus smiles is when she makes a deposit at the bank, or gets another promotion, or forecloses on a farm. Taurus has the reputation of being without sympathy for the less financially well endowed. This is also untrue. Bulls are very aware of and sympathetic to their cash-deprived fellow citizens. Bulls pray they'll never be poor, and they have a reverence for their banks, which they see as the ultimate buffer between themselves and the street.

Still, you'd be shortchanging yourself if you forget that Taurus is into security. Get used to financial practicalities. And become adept at dealing with Taurus's down-to-earth nature by remembering the following:

Don't drop hints. Hints won't penetrate the Taurus psyche. Think of Taurus as a rock: The only way to wear down a rock is gradually with a constant stream of water. Hints won't nick the rock's surface.

→ *Lesson:* Be steady and direct in your communication with Taurus.

Don't play mind games. Since Taurus is not a manipulator, he won't recognize your maneuvering. Save yourself the trouble and the ammunition, while you're at it.

Approach Taurus slowly. Taurus has an appealing steadiness about her communication style. There's a seductive saunter to the Bull's speech patterns. So she doesn't like to be ruffled by a frenetic conversational pace. If you're in a hurry (or if you have a lot of Aries, Aquarius, or Gemini in your chart), slow down—way down.

Keep your feet on the ground. Taurus does. If you don't, Taurus will do it for you. Like an air traffic controller in heavy fog, Taurus makes sure to keep you grounded.

Let Taurus take charge. The Bull is great at keeping things steady and under control. Allow him to indulge his little fetish. Don't worry if you feel as though you've pawned your freedom: You can always redeem it later.

Like a Rock: The Taurus Lover

Do you want a relationship that's smooth and stable? Probably, if you've just come out of the confinement of a relationship with a mind-game champ like Pisces or Scorpio or a flighty piece like Gemini. You look around you for something more restful and predictable, and there stands Taurus. The promise of all that stability is extremely seductive.

You're right, the Taurus lover has the same unspeakable virtues that your Taurus friends or business associates have. The first you'll notice is steadiness. Even if you hadn't just gotten paroled from a relationship with one of the flightier signs, you'd still notice Taurus.

With all this steadiness and reliability, your love relationship has a good chance of lasting. Being a nonparanoid sign, Taurus has few worries, but one concern is the security of her possessions. Taurus wants to keep her assets together. She also wants to make sure that the only things you'll take with you when you leave are what you brought. So don't be surprised if the Bull trots out a prenup, just in case things don't work out. With all this financial anxiety, it follows that if you do split up, the only thing a Taurus lover will worry about is that you'll take her when you leave.

If you're used to wishy-washy, indecisive people, a Taurus lover is as refreshing as floating in a relaxing pool, rising from the water to be enveloped in a soft towel, and feeling the caress of a spring breeze. This seduction of your senses will not only take you off-guard but strip you of it as well.

While you're floating in sensory ecstasy, Taurus makes up his mind. And when he's on the make, nothing deters him. The Bull is headed right for his target, which is you. If you want no part of it, you'd better step aside. It might buy you some time until he picks up your trail.

Taurus Turn-Ons

Now that you've caught Taurus's attention, it's fairly easy to keep it, especially if you keep the following in mind:

Appeal to Taurus's senses. Taurus is vulnerable to atmosphere. Any appeal to the senses will appeal to the Bull. Draw her a bath. Give her a seductive massage with soothing, fragrant oils.

➻ *Lesson:* Make Taurus vulnerable to your desires by appealing to her senses.

Create comfortable surroundings. Remember that Taurus loves comfy surroundings. Taurus lovers may be long on comfort, but no matter how lush or fragrant the surroundings, there's one place Taurus won't go: to extremes.

➻ *Lesson:* Embrace moderation. Taurus also likes to embrace the solidity of tradition.

One way to do this is to talk about family. Taurus likes the security of family. Family carries an implication of permanence and a presumption of continuity that Taurus likes. Be careful though. Taurus isn't easily prodded into one-upmanship, but tread carefully by treating his own family or pedigree with reverence.

If your family is more distinguished than the Bull's, he'll like it. He likes the fact your family came to America when it was made up of colonies instead of states. But don't compare your pedigree to his. For example, don't point out that his family came to America not on the deck of the *Mayflower* but by way of a convict ship bound for Australia.

➳ *Lesson:* Disrespect for Taurus's familial roots will cause the Bull to charge.

Touch Taurus. Taureans are tactile. Touch Taurus first, and hope you're one of the things the Bull wants to touch back.

Admire Taurus's home. You'll get lots of opportunities because you'll be hanging out there a lot. Taurus's favorite place to be is home. If your Taurus is a gadabout, then she's got lots of Gemini in her chart. Sense the tremors of boredom? Well, think of it this way: You'll save lots of money on clothes. You won't need a lot of outfits suitable for making the club circuit.

Encouraging Taurus to Circulate

Sometimes you've just got to get out of the house. Maybe you want to go out to eat at a pricey restaurant. Any time you ask Taurus to part with something—like tangible assets or endless evenings at Chez Taurus—you should set the scene.

The traditional lover-manipulating methods work best: Fill the house with the aroma of comfort foods like homemade bread and set the scene with fragrant wildflowers you've picked from your own garden.

As always, give Taurus plenty of notice. Then draw your Bull's attention to the homey pleasures of your proposed destination.

You: Honey, I was thinking about our going out next weekend.
Taurus: *(with a frown)* But it's so comfortable here.

You: Well, naturally, I love it here. You know that. But I know you're always on the lookout for ways to make our nest more comfortable. I heard the flatware and chair cushions at Chateau Jean-Claude Pierre would be just right for our place.

Of course it's not that simple, so prepare to be persistent. You'll go back and forth a few times, but using these basic tactics, you'll eventually get your way. If this doesn't work, though, volunteer to pick up the tab.

Encouraging Other Adventures

Now that you've gotten your feet wet with evenings out at restaurants, you'd like Taurus to go out even more often. Oddly enough, vacations may be your best bet. Once Taurus gets settled in one place, he likes to stay put.

When you propose a trip, do it gently. Suggest ways to make it more palatable (i.e., inexpensive sounding) to Taurus.

Suggest traveling in the off-season. Have your list of chosen destinations ready, though, or Taurus might take a fancy to exploring Alaska in February or Egypt in August.

You might also want to play on Taurus's liking of domestic comfort. Since hotels can be so impersonal (i.e., expensive), you can talk Taurus into a European vacation by proposing an international house-swap. You can also swap cars. Don't carry this too far, or you might end up wanting to swap lovers, too.

The Taurus Boss

As bosses, people born under the sign of Taurus are custom-built. Financially minded Bulls are part of nature's business brethren and make great stewards of the bottom line. You'll find Taurus in any corporate position but most probably in the front lines when it comes to fielding financial requests. Other more tenderhearted signs like Pisces or harmony-fetishists like Libra are soft touches compared to the cautious Bull. Chances are, less hard-nosed signs learned early the value of having Taurus in charge of the purse strings. With the Taurus boss, the buck does indeed stop here.

Taurus is also in charge of herself, too, so no emotional displays at the office. They're so out of place.

Your Taurus boss is always at work. This can be a drag if you'd rather not be. Like Bulls in your personal life, Taurus bosses are susceptible to their surroundings. Make your office inviting. Decorate it with a few plants: The color of green (whether it's a dollar or a dahlia) is soothing to Taurus. Only when you've set the scene should you approach Taurus with something as outlandish as the possibility of a raise. Here are a few other ways to get along with your Taurus boss.

Stress the Long-Term
Use Taurus-friendly phrases around your boss. The Bull likes to stress the future in business planning. Begin your presentations with phrases like:

- The long-term outlook is . . .
- Over the next few years, look for . . .
- We can expect to see substantial savings over the next ten years

Speak Taurus's Language
It also pays to state just the facts when talking to Taurus. Your boss doesn't indulge in twirly-swirly talks like Gemini or celestial

communications like Pisces. The Bull eats, drinks, and hears with economy.

↦ *Lesson:* Don't embellish your conversations.

Show Your Progress

Let's say you're working on a long-term project. It's taken you months to get to the halfway mark. You've been keeping careful track of your progress on a calendar that's part of your computer software.

Big mistake.

Taurus wants to be able to see your progress. Do you also keep track of your schedule using a month-at-a-glance calendar on your PDA?

Another mistake.

Save your PDA for personal use, and plaster a year-at-a-glance on your wall.

↦ *Lesson:* Before Taurus can believe progress is occurring, he must be able to see it.

Stress Economy When Making Purchases

Let's say you have your eye on some new office equipment. Your computer is running low on memory. It's also ten years old, uses a dot-matrix printer, and is too slow to run the most recently released operating system. Taurus believes in rebuilding an item before replacing it. Taurus is built to last, so expects everything else to be, too. Your computer, for example. Taurus has already installed more memory cards for the computer and has spent as much money adding memory to the computer as it would cost to buy a new one. Being Taurus, your boss doesn't want to replace anything.

You do, though, so plan ahead. Show Taurus a magazine that advertises new computers at cut-rate prices. Let that sink in. Then grab copies of the bills for the extra computer parts and strategically drop them under Taurus's nose. It would also help to attach an adding-machine tape to the bills, which shows the total amount spent on rebuilding the computer (so far). Only then is the stage set for your computer coup:

> You: I was just going over equipment expenses, and I discovered that the department could get a new computer for less than it would cost to fix up the old one.

Now you've caught Taurus's attention. And planted the seed. Be patient while it grows, and you'll eventually end up with a new computer.

Plan Ahead

Do you adore tight deadlines or last-minute conferences? The Bull doesn't.

➼ *Lesson:* Taurus is not into crisis management.

Keep Taurus Informed

A Taurus boss is really nothing to be afraid of. She's not suggestible and can be very reassuring, especially if you've made a mistake (other than being unprepared). She won't pitch a fit; she'll just find a practical solution to your problem.

➼ *Lesson:* Inform Taurus immediately if there's a problem.

Emphasize Savings When Asking for a Raise

Now that you've done such a good job, naturally Taurus will want to reward you—or maybe not. As you may have guessed, this can be a bit tricky. Luck will be on your side if you stack the odds in your favor. First, approach Taurus when he's in a good mood. Taurus is an easygoing sign, but there's one exception: Taurus can get touchy when it's time to assess the department's financial position.

Avoid the Bull when he's in the midst of a financial cycle. If he glances at payables and income on the first and fifteenth of the month, plan to be out of the office. Or out of town, maybe even out of the country.

It's best to emphasize *savings* when proposing a raise. Plan ahead, though. Call attention to an article that tells about the sexy and expensive benefits packages new employees are expecting. Let that sink in, then approach him.

> You: I've studied this carefully, and I think we can save the company some money on staff costs.
>
> Taurus: (*putting down his copy of the* Wall Street Journal) Yes?
>
> You: I've been looking at staff turnover expenses. For what it costs to advertise for a new employee, hire a headhunter, or train a new candidate, we could just give a modest across-the-board raise.

It goes without saying that you will benefit from this benefit. Let the idea sink in.

➻ *Lesson:* Don't push for an answer. Give Taurus a long time to think about it. Maybe even into the next quarter. You don't have the patience? Observe Taurus; maybe some will rub off on you. You'll need it.

Remember that Taurus tantalizes you with feelings of security and will torture you with her tenacity. The steady Taurus plods her way through life; but as a nonmanipulator, she'll never notice your treachery as you try to steer her in the right direction. So emulate Taurus's single-mindedness by plotting and planning, and eventually you'll get what you want. Be patient though; it may take awhile.

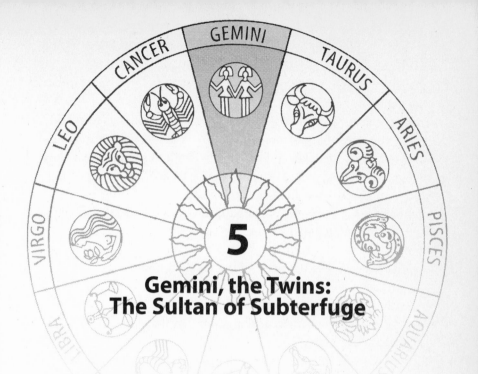

5

Gemini, the Twins:
The Sultan of Subterfuge

Temporary Position Wanted: Smooth operator—skilled in multiple-phone techniques, the Internet, and verbal contortionism—wants to come aboard on a strictly temporary basis. You can reach me on my cell phone for now—by next month, I should be permanently wired.

Gemini sun:	May 22–June 21
Planetary ruler:	Mercury
Gemini Web site:	*www.bllsht/artist*

T alk, talk, talk. Has a Gemini flitted into your orbit? If you're not already a verbal juggler, you'd better toss some linguistic balls in the air, dangle a few participles, and delete the word *permanent* from your vocabulary.

Geminians are splendid listeners. They're the best folks to confide in, and you never have to worry about them telling your secrets. It's not particularly that they're loyal to the death; it's mainly that they forget what you told them as soon as they start another conversation—which is immediately, if not simultaneously.

Look for the Twins floating around anyplace there's talk, schemes, and movement. You'll find Gemini:

- At a meeting of the Book of the Moment Club
- Attached to almost any telephone
- Churning out pithy slogans at an ad agency
- At the appliance store, asking when they'll come out with faster microwave ovens
- On Capitol Hill doing tricky things with the national budget
- Sneaking around on behalf of *The National Enquirer*

You might find Gemini anchoring the nightly news or whispering confidentially over the office water cooler. Wherever he is, whatever he's doing, he's a verbal virtuoso. He's also the warlock of information circulation, which is just Gemini double-talk for a lust for gossip.

The Twins

When manipulating Gemini, always keep in mind her astrological symbol: the Twins. In other words, she has two identities—maybe more. No wonder she can do two things at once. She can also do two people at once. But that's not a problem unless you're married to her.

↬ *Lesson:* Whoever Gemini is today, she'll be someone else tomorrow. Gemini may be versatile, but you're stuck with her foibles. Here's what *not* to expect.

Don't Expect Stability

Gemini uses his two personalities to dart around so fast, you couldn't push his buttons even if you could find them. He doesn't just move and think fast. He also talks fast enough to leave chatskids.

↬ *Lesson:* Expecting a Gemini to be stable is like counting on a politician to keep promises—naive and a complete waste of time.

Don't Expect Commitment

Say you want to pin Gemini down about something important. The conversation will go something like this:

> You: So, Gem, what do you want to be when you grow up? If you grow up, that is?
> Gemini: *(eagerly)* Well, I thought I'd . . . (She breezes into an answer with such eloquence that she talks herself hoarse.)

When Gemini is finished, do you feel satisfied she's given you a firm answer? You shouldn't. Gemini just spent the whole conversation wriggling, squirming, and speaking in a very learned way that hides the fact she hasn't committed to anything at all.

↬ *Lesson:* To Gemini, words are to be climbed over, hidden behind, and threaded onto hooks as bait. So you're going to have to learn to use her own bait against her.

The Verbal Arsenal

You can get your way with Gemini—if you're good with words. Here's the best way to use words when psyching out the Twins. Or, to translate into Twin-speak, how to be verbally expedient in achieving your goals with Gemini.

Use Words as Weapons

Gemini uses words as verbal darts, and he expects you to throw a few back. Entice him with words like *quick, temporary,* and *flexible.* And you can really blast him into the stratosphere with *long-term, routine,* and *stable.*

Know the Gemini Vocabulary

Do your palms sweat at the sight of a dictionary? Do you tremble when touching a thesaurus? You can still get your way with Gemini by relying on words—her words. Memorize these definitions from the Gemini dictionary:

- *Clock*—A primitive torture device used to force Geminis to be on time; believed to have been invented by the Marquis de Sade
- *Commitment*—A state in which one is pinned down; often leads to boredom and certain death
- *Job*—An endeavor that pays small amounts of money in exchange for sacrificing huge amounts of free time; usually requires a commitment (see earlier definition)

These words are no-nos. Don't use them.

Beware Gemini Bullshit

Gemini is dangerous. How can that be? you ask. She's so agreeable. And charming. Not to mention nimble and persuasive.

That's why she's dangerous.

Gemini will dazzle you with tricks while she weasels her way out of trouble and into your confidence. Watch out!

Beware the Gemini Charm

The Twins are slick. Cagey. Clever. They can talk a guy into leaving his wife before he's even gotten married. They can also talk you into doing things you had no intention of doing.

➥ *Lesson:* Gemini is expert at saying things that sound vague but in reality are meaningless. He can slant, fabricate, and improvise with the zeal of a thousand Hollywood agents. This talent for felicitous phrasing has given Gemini a reputation for insincerity. This, as any Libra will tell you, is unfair. You don't have to sneer at Gemini glibness. But you don't have to fall for it, either.

Beware the Gemini Sideways Shuffle

Lightning-fast Gemini may seem to dart around indiscriminately, but she is capable of great focus. Especially when you want to focus on something important. The Twins can sense a serious conversation a light-year away. For example, maybe you'd like to have a little chat about the hundred dollars Gemini owes you.

Gemini is perfectly happy to talk it over. She sits down.

You: I hate to be a nag, but do you remember the time I loaned you money when you had to replace a tire on your car?

Gemini: *(smiling brightly)* Of course. And I was so grateful; you know how I hate to be stuck in one place for long. Speaking of, do you remember when I visited Prague and was stuck there for three days?

Then Gemini regales you with a rambling conversation about foreign currency exchange rates, the stability of Eastern Europe, and what fun it would be to travel in South America.

Gemini: *(glancing at her watch ten minutes later)* Is that the time? Wow. It was great talking to you, let's get together again soon.

She's wriggled out the door before you can reel her back in.

➥ *Lesson: A* Gemini can change subjects as fast as she can change identities.

Beware the Gemini Promise

You: Will you pick up my dry cleaning?

Gemini: I'll be happy to.

You wait patiently. But don't wait too long. By the time he makes it to the laundry, your clothes will be out of fashion.

And it's no good being pissed off. He really meant to do it; something just distracted him on the way.

➥ *Lesson:* The Gemini motto is "Promise anything; then forget to do it."

Beware the Gemini Euphemism

If you want the relief of forthright communication, debate an Aries. The linguistically limber Gemini communicates indirectly. Forewarned is forearmed.

He says, *"Great vintage clothes you're wearing."*
Interpretation: He can't help noticing your jacket is two seasons out of date.

She says, *"Of course I'm listening; you know how much I respect your judgment."*
Interpretation: Gemini has developed selective hearing; she has no respect whatsoever for your judgment.

He says, *"Fred's a true Renaissance man."*
Interpretation: Fred has done everything from waiting tables to cleaning sewers to selling junk bonds, and he's married to three women at the same time.

She says, *"You're as intelligent as you are attractive."*
Interpretation: This could mean absolutely anything.

Gemini's Achilles' Heel: Change

Craving it, chasing it, creating it. If you're around a Gemini who won't change, you'd better check his pulse and sell-by date. He may very well be dead.

Gemini's changeability is one reason it's so hard to keep him from flitting all over the place. You can still get your way, though. Here's how to get him to flit in the direction *you* want him to go.

Make boring things sound exciting. To Gem, boredom's the result of restriction. And restriction reminds her of jail and other depressing places that affect reception on her cell phone. Try this when sending Gemini on a cramped, ten-hour transatlantic flight: "Just think! You have all that time to read and watch movies!"

Set Gemini's clocks forward. A moronic technique, but it's the only way you'll trick Gemini into punctuality.

Derail Gemini's plans. Gemini loves to make plans—so he can break them. Say you're on a shopping trip with Gemini. He plans to browse the electronics store, but you want to look at clothes. Pretend you're dying to look at the latest high-definition TV. But as you approach the window of a boutique, stop and say, "Look! Isn't that a cunningly constructed mannequin?" Walk in the store. Dollars to doughnuts, Gemini will follow you.

The Sultan of Subterfuge: The Gemini Lover

Are you frightened by fickleness? If you're involved with a Gemini, get used to it. Sometimes he's so fickle, he's promiscuous. The Twins' idea of an intimate relationship is to have a deep thing going with two or three really witty people.

I'll say no more in the interests of astrological impartiality, but you can at least be sure of this.

➥ *Lesson:* One twin will be faithful to you at all times.

Gemini, more than any other sign, is attracted to people like himself. That's because Gemini is a dual sign, and he's used to seeing his own reflection—even when he's alone and without a mirror.

Selling Yourself to the Gemini Lover

Be flirtatious. Gemini likes to flirt even more than Scorpio likes to have sex. Gem will flirt with you, your grandfather, and the cop who ticketed her for speeding. If you don't flirt back, she'll think you're not interested.

Be unpredictable. The only thing Gem hates more than boredom is routine. Try changing plans at the last minute. Go to a new restaurant. See a movie in a foreign language (preferably in a foreign country). Dye your hair. Change your address. You get the picture.

Be fun. Addicted to misery? Don't trash your Gemini love affair with it. Share it with a Capricorn; he won't even notice. Be playful to keep Gemini tuned in. Have you bored him to yawning-point? He'll disappear before you ever see him yawn twice.

Adopt a Gemini persona. Because Gemini's such a quick-change artist with his multiple identities, she's also into multiplicity in love affairs. Yes, Gemini can be into multiple affairs, but there's an easy way to satisfy this urge without the interference of other lovers. Indulge in sexual role-playing: As long as Gemini wants to make love with different people, why not make all of them you?

Pretend you're a college cheerleader. Or a Chippendale dancer who's making a house call. Gemini will love it.

➻ *Lesson:* Try on various personalities when bedding down a Gemini. If you try on different personalities, Gemini might try being focused on you.

Be sexually adventurous—mentally. A Gemini lover's idea of adventurousness shouldn't scare you. He doesn't necessarily expect you to explore romantic opportunities outside the relationship. He does, however, expect you to explore places beyond the boundaries of your imagination. Are you normally private about your fantasies? Embarrassed, even? Then you're in luck with a Gemini lover; you can feel okay about having fantasies *and* talk about them.

Gemini likes the *idea* of kinky sex but not necessarily the reality. If you've ever wondered what it would be like to install a trapeze in the bedroom, dress up in leather undergarments, or raid the erotic literature section of your local bookstore, just talk to Gemini about it. The great thing is you won't actually have to follow up on it.

How to Turn Off a Gemini Lover

There are a few things you shouldn't do to your Gemini lover.

- Don't complain about the yard-high stack of books on the bedside table
- Don't hide his car keys
- Don't switch the dust jacket from her thesaurus onto a guide for responsible financial planning
- Don't unplug his modem
- Don't mention the word *marriage* (The only time Gemini will go for a word like *marriage* is if it's preceded by the word *open*.)

Keeping the Gemini Lover Interested

➡ *Lesson:* The only way to keep a Gemini interested is to be interesting.

Be multifaceted. Act as multifaceted as possible without risking a diagnosis of schizophrenia. Gem covets variety. Trot out all your interests, preferably at the same time. Quote Tolstoy while you're skydiving. Talk about quantum physics while tossing together a gourmet meal. Don't worry that she'll think you're inconsistent. Show your constancy to a Taurus.

Be polygamous. You might as well be. Gemini is.

The Gemini Boss

Is your boss impatient with pesky details? Is he paranoid about management shrinking his expense account to six figures? Is he out of the office most of the time?

Other times, does he pick so hard at your grammar that you've had traumatic grade-school flashbacks? Does he red-line extravagances like

This means he wants you to take him to the airport tomorrow. It also means you should check out the flight details beforehand, like the terminal and the gate.

> Boss: Here are my ideas for adding a basketball court to our waiting room. The details are there; just summarize them.

He's handed you pages and pages of sketches, scribbles, and cryptic jottings topped off with exclamation points. This means the only way to cope is to become a Virgo.

♊ ♊ ♊

Geminis are the quick-change artists of the zodiac, and they have an unfair abundance of charm. They also have the ability to use charm to weasel their way out of trouble. The Gemini also talks fast and moves fast. This penchant for flitting around can be a problem when you want to shoot him. Just hold onto your ammunition, and outwit him by using his own words against him. Brush up on your persuasion skills, and with practice you can manipulate the Twins, one at a time.

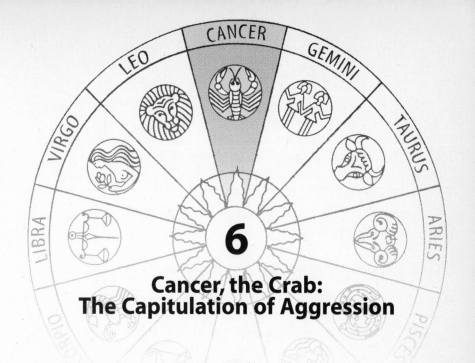

6

Cancer, the Crab:
The Capitulation of Aggression

Ravenous? You've pulled into the right driveway. Slip off your shoes and come into my parlor. Pull up a chair, and I'll set the table and an atmosphere for tea and sympathy. I'll share everything—except my secrets and you. You'll be so comfortable, you won't even notice I took your car keys.

Cancer sun:	June 22–July 23
Planetary ruler:	The Moon
Cancer Web site:	*www.easily/fd*

You've entered a room filled with warmth, the aroma of freshly baked bread, and the crackling of bursting logs in the fireplace. It reminds you of how much you long for your favorite drink, a hot buttered rum. Almost like magic, Cancer greets you with a smile and the steaming beverage you crave.

Have you floated into an enchanted place where desires are fulfilled merely by thinking about them? This paradise feels like home: what home should have been, the home of your dreams. You're right. It is a dream. It's also a trap.

Welcome to the Cancerian cabana. You can check out whatever time you like, but Cancer will never let you leave.

Where to Find Cancer

It's hard to get a grip on the sympathetic and secretive Crab. Not only will he skid sideways to avoid your grasp, but Cancer is also secretive about anything he considers personal. And he thinks everything is personal. Cancer may be quiet, but you can still find him:

- Cooking a good meal
- Offering a shoulder to cry on
- Looking for a shoulder to cry on
- Beating around the bush
- Avoiding an issue

Life with a Cancer can be a bit puzzling. Cancer is usually such a gentle, considerate soul. Then she astonishes you by pricking you with conversational jabs.

For example, Cancer knows you're sensitive about the ten pounds you've put on over the past few months. And then ever-sensitive

Cancer turns on you and says, "I ordered some new slacks for you, dear. They're the next size larger."

→ *Lesson:* Get used to Cancerian sniping.

How to Get What You Want from Cancer

Cancer is the caretaker of the zodiac. He is always there when you need him. So giving. So loving. So irritating.

The Crab needs to give. He also has deep emotional needs and a great need to have them met. How do you know what he needs? By observing what he does for you and doing the same for him. Unnerve him by outnurturing him. Caring and sharing: that's how Cancer gets you into his debt. Follow suit, and nail him with nurturing.

Be Sensitive to Cancer

Cancer approaches all relationships emotionally, whether they involve friends, lovers, or bosses. She'll be more susceptible to you if you're sensitive, too. Send her a birthday card. Return her library book before it's overdue.

→ *Lesson:* Be considerate to Cancer.

Nurture Cancer

Remember the day Cancer took you out to lunch to console you on the first anniversary of your divorce? Maybe Cancer had a car wreck recently. Send him a basket of bestsellers and cherry-loaf bread to ease his convalescence.

→ *Lesson:* When life throws Cancer a curve, caress him with kindness.

Cancer's Achilles' Heel: The Need to Be Needed

Cancer needs to feed you when you're famished and soothe you when you're distressed. Cancers are pleasers, and they need to be needed. So please need Cancer. Take advantage of it; the benefits can be great. Cancers genuinely like to pamper, cosset, and otherwise spoil the people in their lives. To be the recipient of all this loving care is one of your duties. Don't even think of turning down Cancer's cosseting, or you could get ground into the dirt by Cancer's Achilles' heel.

How to Sidestep Cancerian Quicksand: Cancer Don'ts

Cancer is fully functional and comes with attachments included. His main attachment is to you. You probably think this means you can do no wrong. Well, think again. Noting the following don'ts will smooth life with the Crab.

Don't Hurt Cancer's Feelings

Yes, this probably sounds like "Don't get cold in a blizzard." Cancer is tuned into you and maneuvers her way through your mind using sensitivity sonar. This means she knows what makes you tick. She also knows how to tick you off. And she'll do it to punish you after you've hurt her feelings.

Cancer must be miffed, because she's sniping at you so much you wish your flak jacket were handy. Her sly comments about your weight gain and tight trousers are pissing you off.

What did you do wrong? Nothing that you can think of: You didn't forget your anniversary. You also remembered to water Cancer's palm tree, a legacy from her godmother.

Think back to this morning and what you said as you left to drop the kids off at school: "You sure do look sexy in that outfit." Most people consider that a compliment. Cancer considers it an implication that she doesn't look sexy in any other outfit. Or, worse, she has to keep her clothes on to be considered sexy.

↬ *Lesson:* Be careful what you say and how you say it. It will save trouble and maybe even a life.

Don't Be Unavailable

You're going on a trip, and the thought of being without you is shredding Cancer's nerves. Be accessible even though you're gone. Leave a phone number where you can be reached; post a copy of your itinerary on the refrigerator. And while you're gone, buy Cancer a souvenir. Your thoughtfulness will smooth the way for your next trip. It also proves you thought about him while you were away.

↬ *Lesson:* If you must be away from Cancer, stay in touch.

Don't Be Direct

Cancers already give so much, you're ashamed to ask for one more thing—like a direct answer. Well, don't ask, because Cancer can't give you one.

Manipulating Cancer can lead you into psychological quicksand. You've been lured by the insidious Cancerian traits of sensitivity, understanding, and nurturing. Cancer's sixth sense makes him one of nature's manipulators, because he knows how to get to you. And once he gets you, he'll want to possess you.

Like all astrological signs who are lucky enough to be born manipulators, Cancer is an expert at using covert tactics while protecting his back. So, protect yourself as you manipulate him. Be observant, be aware, and be alert to his body language, because it's always different from his spoken language. Observe what Cancer *does;* ignore what he says. Confuse and confound him with soothing words, and then launch your frontal attack. It's the one place he's not expecting it.

Dealing with Cancer, the Covert Communicator

Does your Cancer know what she needs, and does she ask for it? Does she confront emotional issues head-on? If you answered "yes" to these questions, the person you're dealing with is masquerading as a Cancer.

You can't manipulate somebody if you don't know what she wants. With Cancer, you're in trouble if you're untrained in the art of covert communication.

Cancer is understanding. She instinctively knows what you need and lavishes you with loving concern. But she's as much of a mystery as are her longings. She won't let you get a grip on her, and she can't get a grip on what she wants to say, much less say it.

Unfortunately, Cancer expects you to read her thoughts, anticipate her needs, and fulfill them—all without benefit of a conversation. These expectations could lead to frustration and an unsightly illegal domestic incident.

There are two reasons to meet Cancer's needs. First, addressing her needs is the best way to persuade her to meet *your* needs. Second, you must reckon with Cancerian desires, or Cancer will take a trip into misery and drag you along. Short of becoming a psychic or a psychiatrist or a psychiatric patient, there is a solution to this conundrum. There are two ways to deal with the Crab's needs: learn to decode her nonverbal hints and then dodge them until you have time to cope.

How to Perceive Cancer's Needs

Cancer does not communicate verbally and is astrologically incapable of talking and asking for what he wants at the same time.

So you'll have to decipher what he's trying to communicate. Read on to learn how to find out what Cancer wants.

Observe Cancer's actions. Cancer is polishing the hardwood floor. This is normal, but the fact that he keeps polishing the same spot is unusual. So is the fact that this spot is now spotless, and there are much dustier corners to be cleaned.

What's special about this part of the parquet? You're standing next to it. Cancer's attention to the floor near you means he wants attention *from* you. This is your cue to look at Cancer. As soon as you do, he glances at the "Art and Culture" section of the newspaper, then back to you. Cancer just dropped a hint. Pick it up.

> You: (leafing through the paper) Hey, would you like to go to the movies and see the Casablanca revival?
>
> Cancer: What a good idea.

➥ *Lesson:* Pick up Cancer's hints by observing his actions.

How to Defer Dealing with Cancer's Needs

Usually you don't mind playing charades with Cancer, but it takes time and you don't have any. Show you're aware of Cancer's needs without meeting them. This action will reassure her that you'll take care of things later.

Forestall Cancer's present demands by thanking him for a favor he did for you in the past. You've heard Cancer is having marital problems and wants to talk about them. You'd like to sympathize, but don't have time. But you do have time to say how much you appreciate him.

For example, maybe Cancer gave you a lift home when you had car trouble after a trying day at the gym.

> You: It was so nice of you to rescue me after I blew my radiator

hose last week.

Cancer: *(smiling)* I'm just glad I was there to drive you home.

↣ *Lesson:* Tell Cancer you appreciate him. Gratitude is great currency, and you can use it to cash in later.

Use sympathetic phrases while blowing her off. Maybe Cancer is complaining about the shortage of tufted toilet tissue again. Respond with sympathetic sounding but noncommittal phrases such as "How trying," "I can sympathize," or the ever-popular "What a nuisance."

↣ *Lesson:* Sympathize with Cancer's concerns without doing anything about them.

Ignore Cancer. He'll get over it. Eventually.

The Cancer Lover

What heavenly bliss that Cancer lovers hug you often. They always kiss you good night and good morning and tell you they love you. In the winter, they tiptoe over frosty lawns to pick up the newspaper so you don't have to. In the summer, they surprise you with a beach towel and membership to the neighborhood swimming pool. If this weren't hard enough to take, they're good cooks, too.

Tonight, you're getting the full treatment: a wonderful meal in beautiful surroundings. Sumptuous delicacies made exactly as you crave them: the asparagus steamed to crispness, the chicken grilled yet juicy, and the Sauvignon Blanc chilled in a silver bucket moist with condensation. It's a beautiful night, and you sigh with contentment.

Then you hear another sigh—from Cancer. And that's all you hear, all night. You're getting the silent treatment, and you don't even know what you've done wrong.

Are you sure it wasn't a crab that sneaked into the Garden of Eden?

One problem with Cancers is they do everything indirectly.

Another problem with Cancers is that they're nurturing. They already give so much that you feel sheepish asking for anything more. Time away from home, for example. Or a solo trip to the movies. Go ahead and ask, but there's a price: guilt. Guilt is a Cancerian specialty. Get used to it.

Because of the many benefits of life with a Cancer lover, it's only realistic to expect a few rough spots. Here are a few problems you can expect and the best way to deal with them.

Appreciate Cancer

It's the day after your romantic dinner and Cancer still hasn't spoken to you. When did Cancer stop speaking and start sighing? What's wrong? It could be any number of things. Be as observant as Cancer. Look around the house and flip through your memory banks. You notice a few things Cancer could be upset about:

- You left the cap off the shampoo
- You let milk dry on the cappuccino machine
- You used a broom to sweep the floor instead of a dust mop
- Yesterday, you asked Cancer to do his own laundry
- Last night, you said Cancer didn't have to cook and that Chinese take-out would be fine with you
- You—Stop right there. Cancer started sighing right after dinner. Cancer thinks you don't like his cooking. And you don't appreciate him.

➻ *Lesson:* Compliment Cancer's thoughtfulness.

Embrace Cancer's Possessiveness

You've just gotten home, and Cancer is pleased to see you.

Cancer: Wouldn't it be nice to drive to the country with friends and have a moonlight picnic?

You're tired. You've had a long day, you were stuck in rush-hour traffic, and your feet hurt. You want to tuck up in bed and read a book.

You: *(after outlining your ratty day)* I'm going to bed early. But go ahead and enjoy yourself.

You expect to hear Cancer's car rev up as you bend back the covers of a good mystery novel. Instead, you hear Cancer tiptoeing up the stairs. As Cancer curls up next to you and your book, you remember this:
↠ *Lesson:* Cancer is possessive. Of her bank account, her territory as defined by a picket fence or the walls of her corner office, and of you—especially of you. Don't expect time alone.

Get Used to Guilt Trips

Cancer is acting withdrawn, so you ask what's wrong. Cancer doesn't reply. So you decide to guess. You're starting to pick up Cancer's signals and sense a guilt trip on the horizon. Yes, you know you've sinned, but you're not keen to do penance; besides, you've left your hair shirt at the cleaners along with Cancer's favorite dress slacks. The following will help you spot this Cancerian tactic and show you how to react.

You: Are you upset because I forgot to recharge the battery on the portable phone?

Cancer remains silent, and you try again.

You: *(searching your conscience as you look around the room)* Is it because I forgot to water the bouquet of wildflowers you brought home? Or is it because my car broke down and I missed the company picnic?

Cancer: It's nothing.

It is something, and you know it, so you search the house later. Everything is the same, except for an envelope resting against the flower vase. You open the envelope and pull out a card, which is blank and unsigned. Now you understand what's bothering Cancer.

You: *(blushing with guilt while whispering in Cancer's ear)* I'm sorry I forgot to write a thank-you note for the flowers.

Cancer: *(with a sigh of relief)* It's okay. I understand.

Cancer's reaction should remind you.

➦ *Lesson:* Don't take Cancer for granted. Or if you do, thank her later for the nice things she did today.

Yes, Cancer lovers can be exasperating. Cancer is so hard to figure out and sometimes terrifyingly possessive. But maybe you should be flattered Cancer thinks you're worth holding onto.

When you're feeling crabby yourself, look around you for reminders of Cancer's thoughtfulness: the wildflowers or the James Bond book you read while curled up with Cancer. Then think back, and recall the aroma of the hot buttered rum from last winter.

Then look forward to the annual croquet party Cancer gives each spring: evenings garnished with mood music, mimosas made with freshly squeezed orange juice, and the feel of soft, warm breezes.

Reread your croquet rule book, and remind yourself of a certain croquet term: a rush on the ultimate. Sounds like life with a Cancer lover. Cancer doesn't choose croquet parties for nothing.

The Cancer Boss

You're the proud employee of a Cancer boss. A Cancer boss is just as nurturing as your Cancerian friends or lovers. She's the creator of your career environment. Your office will have homey touches. Couches, if there's room, or at least cushy chairs. She's sensitive to the office's environment, both physical and emotional, and wants things to run smoothly. She wants the office atmosphere to be relaxed, and the staff to feel happy, comfortable, and appreciated so you can do your job.

Engrave in your day planner the phrase *so you can do your job*. Cancer isn't in business just for the nurturing experience. Cancer gives at home, but she doesn't give at the office for nothing. She's in it for the cash, and don't forget it.

➟ *Lesson:* Don't forget to do your job. If you relax in the office's cradle of comfort and neglect your duties, you'll hear the thump of a falling pink slip on your office floor.

Cancer nurtures employees on the job because she's considerate. But also so it'll translate to the bottom line. Cancer's financial statements may be on floppy disk or in a leather-bound, green-paged ledger. But she has memorized the numbers on her balance sheet and income statement, and she knows precisely what her assets are.

➟ *Lesson:* Be one of Cancer's assets, or be out of a job.

To remind your boss of how valuable you are, follow these suggestions:

Save Cancer money. You've discovered a way to save money. Show Cancer you can negotiate a deal that saves money in the long run and back it up with hard figures.

> You: *(talking to Cancer while leafing through the ledger)* If we order supplies in bulk, we'll get a quantity discount. It'll also save time, which cuts down on staff costs.
>
> Cancer: Great idea. Let's do it.

Bring problems directly to your Cancer boss. Unlike Cancer friends or lovers, Cancer bosses deal with issues directly. But like all Crabs, he is sensitive, and you don't want to worry him with problems you assume you should deal with yourself.

For example, an outstanding account is due in thirty days, and this is day twenty-eight. You decide not to point it out to your boss unless the bill is overdue. Bad choice. Cancer tackles you about it in a subtle way.

> You: *(with a blush of shame as Cancer waggles the invoice in front of you)* It's not due yet. I can call the customer tomorrow, and the bill will be paid on time.
>
> Cancer: *(rebuking you gently)* It's too bad you didn't send out a reminder two weeks ago. Then the money would be in the bank now.

➻ *Lesson:* Don't procrastinate. If you have questions, ask directly and immediately—especially if it has to do with money.

Deal with irate customers. Cancer likes things to run smoothly. Crisis management is not her style, but it's not because she can't handle it. It's because she doesn't like emotional upsets. Either deal with them yourself or don't let customers get irate.

Invite your Cancer boss home to dinner. Your Cancer boss is just as vulnerable to domesticity as your Cancer friends or lovers. Cancer's own home is sacred. By inviting him to yours, you'll show him he's accepted. He'll be touched when you extend the invitation. Try something like this:

> You: Would you like to come to dinner on Saturday? It's casual, just a small dinner party. Then maybe we can watch a video after the kids have gone to bed.

Cancer: I'd like that very much. May I bring the wine?

Clever Cancer lures you into his orbit with the come-hither of contentment. Hang onto the thought of "contentment" because sensitive Cancer never approaches issues—or you—directly. Have you ever stood next to a smoker and worried about the effects of passive smoking? Try standing next to a Cancer and feeling the effects of passive aggression. Step carefully when manipulating the Crab, or you'll have to answer to Cancer.

7

Leo, the Lion:
The Dictator Diva

Casting Call: Open auditions being held for the drama of my life. Don't try to compete for star billing. Supporting roles only. Apply at the stage door.

Leo sun:	July 24–August 23
Planetary ruler:	The Sun
The Leo Web site:	*www.kssmyass/now*

I magine you're at the opera, soaking up the atmosphere. The music is dramatic, the costumes sumptuous. The building is lavishly appointed on a grand scale. Keep this in mind, because that's what life is like with Leo. When the Dictator Diva sings, "Me, me, me," it's not just a vocal exercise.

Command Performance

In Leo's opera of existence, remember to treat Leo as the star. (You could also treat him like the director, the producer, the composer, the librettist, and every other major player in Leo's Opera of Life, but this can get unwieldy.) Leo's ego needs top billing, so put his name on your marquee in large lighted letters—with glitter.

Pay Attention to Leo

There's a reason this sign is ruled by the sun. Leo finds it delightful (not to mention handy) that the sun is the center of the solar system. How can anyone ignore the center of the universe? The first time you do, it will be your last.

Let Leo Take Center Stage

Leo likes to talk. Just stand in the wings, keep your mouth shut, and let her do the talking. Later, Leo will reminisce, "I just love conversing with so and so. He's such a brilliant conversationalist."

Praise Leo

Leo gets off on praise. One of the reasons Leo does *anything* is so someone will notice. And applaud. Loudly. While clapping, think to yourself, "Stroke, stroke." This is helpful for the following reasons.

1. That's what slaves say with each pull of the oars to which they've been chained (by Leo).
2. It will remind you that the Lion needs to be stroked if you have any hope of taming him.

Give the Lion a compliment such as, "Yes, Leo, you wield that credit card extremely well. Almost like a professional." Imagine what Leo expects when he really does accomplish something. Know how to genuflect?

 Leo's Achilles' Heel: FLATTERY
Does using CAPITAL LETTERS seem overdone? It is, and Leos can be. When flattering the diva in your life, you may feel as if you're overdoing it, too. Don't. It's impossible.

When Leo hears the saying, "Less is more," she roars. Leo thinks *more* is more. When paying compliments, you should, too.

What's wrong with the following compliment?

You: You're so capable, bright, and nice-looking.

This is the sort of compliment that would send most people reeling. Leo didn't even hear you. Try saying something like this:

You: You're absolutely indispensable. Brilliant. And incredibly gorgeous.

Better.

Making Overtures to Leo: The Leo Bribe

Yes, flattery always works with Leo. But maybe you're getting bored with it. Try bribery instead. Presenting goodies to Leo is good in two ways. First, Leo likes it. Not only will he love the actual gift giving, afterward he'll be reminded of how considerate you are each time he looks at it.

It's good for you, too. An offering to Leo is a gift that keeps on giving. To you, that is. It pays dividends.

When shopping for gifts to buy Leo lovers, friends, or employers, get used to asking sales reps, "What can you show me that's the latest in ostentation?" Never buy from a discount store. Leo will be unimpressed with your bargain-hunting abilities. Save that for your Taurus and Capricorn buddies who think discounts are dashing.

↝ *Lesson:* When buying gifts, remember that bigger is better; almost vulgar is perfect. Pay attention to the way the gift is presented, too. Leo is one of the few signs for whom the wrapping is as important as the gift itself. Here are a few gift suggestions:

- For the literary Leo, never buy a paperback. Purchase a hardcover coffee-table book, preferably as big as the coffee table itself.
- For the corporate Leo, get any office accessory that you can have engraved or embossed with her name. Not just initials, the full name. In fact, make up an extra middle name and see if Leo corrects you. Bet she won't. (And it's never too much to add those confirmation and family names.)
- For the blue-collar Leo, buy an electroplated gold ratchet set in a nifty, personalized tool box.
- Get a Leo teacher a tape recorder. The Lion loves to lecture. Now he can lecture to the tape recorder and not bore other people.

- If you find yourself in doubt, buy a camera. For yourself. Snap Leo's picture often, and give her double prints. And enlargements.

The Lover's Duet: The Leo Lover

Using "Leo" and "lover" in the same sentence is redundant. (As any picky Virgo will tell you, which is also redundant.) Your Leo is always in love—if not with you, at least with the person he sees in the mirror.

All-purpose manipulation tactics like flattery and bribery will serve you well. Serving is something you'd better get used to. You'll do a lot of it around Leo. Here's some romantic fine-tuning.

Attracting Leo

You see Leo across a crowded room (it's crowded with the ever-present Leo entourage). Leo is the center of attention—how could it be otherwise? The Lion is holding the conversational floor; besides, she's left an open tab at the bar and everyone in the place knows it.

After you've spotted Leo, approach.

Adore Leo

➺ *Lesson:* Leo always craves respect. And recognition. Try using the following opening conversational gambit to persuade Leo to ignore the rest of the entourage and focus on you.

> You: Didn't I see you in a small part in the film *The Canterbury Tales* starring Leonardo DiCaprio?

Here are the keys to this tactic:

- Your assumption that Leo is a celebrity
- The mention of theatricals of any kind

- Your assumption that Leo looks like the kind of person who's on a first-name basis with Leonardo
- You're crediting Leo with having actually read *The Canterbury Tales*

At this point, Leo will say, "Well, no, actually." But he'll smile confidentially, as if to say that playing in *The Canterbury Tales* is the sort of thing he *might* have done.

Now Leo will ask what you do.

Bestow a dazzling smile and say, "I work for a big law firm downtown." Even if you're a partner who specializes in contracts, make it sound as if you're an underling. Leo can't stand being upstaged.

Leo's eyes brighten. "Oh, I used to share office space with a lawyer. You know the four elements that go into making a valid contract? First, there's capacity, which is . . ."

Listen attentively.

➻ *Lesson:* While Leo talks, all you need to say is nothing.

You might vary that a little with "Really?" or "You don't say," accompanied by ever-more amazed and admiring raises of the eyebrows. This way, you make Leo think she knows more about something than you do.

Leo is bound to be impressed by your adoration. She's sized you up as a possible consort—if not for life, at least for a quick lay. Lucky you. Now what?

Leo Turn-Ons

Now that you've attracted Leo, how do you keep Mr. or Ms. Lion interested? The best way is to make your courtship as romantic as possible. Leo likes romance.

Cultivate courtly manners. Leo believes in the niceties of romance.

If you're the guy, open the Lioness's door. Help her on with her coat. And yes, it goes without saying that you should escort Leo yourself. Only Aries, Aquarius, or Sagittarius types would suggest meeting you at the restaurant or theater.

Choose a romantic setting for your date. Take Leo to the theater, a movie, an art gallery. Anyplace where people are acting. Leo identifies with drama.

Or go to a glitzy see-and-be-seen restaurant. Make sure you have a bottle of champagne waiting at the table. Eat your meal with one hand, and indulge in public displays of affection with the other.

When you've finished dinner, pay with a platinum credit card, not cash. You probably won't have a choice after Leo has run her fingers through your wallet. She's not exactly sure what cash looks like, so it's unlikely to impress her. After dinner, go to a romantic nightspot, order the most expensive cocktail on the menu, lean forward and say, "Tell me about you."

Leo will. In depth.

More Leo Turn-Ons

Keep the romance going in your love relationship with Leo. The relationship will go more smoothly if you act as if it's a love affair, even if you're married or shacked up. Especially if you're married or shacked up.

Remember Leos can be domineering and must be the center of attention. Also keep the following in mind:

Don't compete. It's not that Leo can't stand competition; it's simply that he doesn't want any. In matters of career, for example, by all means trot out your impressive profession and credentials. Leo likes high-flying people. However, it had better not be Leo's profession, too. If it is, downplay your accomplishments.

Don't slight Leo. Since Leo is so sensitive to being ignored, it's easy to slight her. For instance, maybe you were supposed to call Leo before lunch. Your day was a collision of the trivial with the time consuming: Faxes flew, and you had to interrupt your day to rescue a friend whose car stalled and deal with a kitten who swallowed an earring. It's now half-past four. The phone rings and, as you pick up the receiver, you suddenly remember you were supposed to call Leo.

Before the Lion has a chance to roar, prevent it with a phrase that makes her think she's your first priority.

Try saying things like: "I was just thinking of you," or "I was just dialing your number."

No, you're not lying. You were thinking of Leo. You don't have to tell her what you were thinking.

Seduce Leo with gifts. Yes, we've already touched on the wisdom of bribing Leo, but it bears repeating here. Leos love gifts. Gifts will get you out of trouble if you've been naughty. It has other perks, too. Like sex.

With all the flattery, gifts, and romantic evenings, you'll certainly end up in the Leo bedroom.

Don't be surprised to find a mirror on the bedroom ceiling. Just don't block Leo's view.

Keeping Leo Interested

Now that you're in the chorus of Leo's operatic life, get ready for a reversal of tactics. During courtship, Leo's manners were quaint, even courtly. Remember the way Leo always opened doors for you? Now, *you're* the one who has to flatter Leo. To keep him happy, you should:

Obey Leo's commands. When Leo gives an order say, "Yes, yes, yes." Leo likes lip service. Then do whatever the hell you want.

Ask nicely. Leo thinks certain people were put on this earth to do menial tasks. Leo is not one of those people. Want Leo to do something tedious, like dealing with the bank statement? Without thinking, you plunge right in and ask.

> You: I want you to balance the checkbook.
> Leo: No!
> You: Will you help me balance the checkbook?
> Leo: No!

As you see, this technique is getting no results. Try this:

> You: I've gotten this checkbook in such a mess. Will you look at it? I'd really value your contribution.
> Leo: *(magnanimously)* Give it to me. *I'll* take care of it.

Always use BIG words. To please Leo, use big words. No, not words with more than one syllable. We're talking words with shades of grandiosity like *grand, huge, massive, impressive, best*—you get the picture.

For example, when Leo tells you about his idea for getting ahead at work, say, "That's a grand idea," or "I think that's a huge step forward."

Getting Out of Sticky Situations

Love relationships with Leo aren't all champagne and mattress-dancing. Here are a couple of tricky situations and the best ways to cope with them.

Handling Leo's pouting. Leo will do one of two things when pissed off: roar or pout. Roars are best as Leo pouts are deafening. And Leo is liable to freeze you out just when you want to show off her sparkling sociable side. Like, for instance, when you're entertaining your boss or a VIP. Leo is sitting next to your boss at dinner. Your future at the company is hanging on a good impression. The boss is trying hard, and if Leo doesn't engage in conversation soon, the boss will think you're a dead loss. Like your Leo.

Your Boss: *(to Leo)* I understand you run an art gallery.
    Leo: Yes.

Your boss fidgets and looks around for somebody who'll talk. It's time for you to step in.

You: *(from across the table)* I love art. Especially the Renaissance Impressionists. Don't you, darling?
Leo: Renaissance Impressionists? There's no such thing. You don't know what you're talking about. The Impressionist movement . . .

In her eagerness to correct your mistake, Leo forgets to pout. The social situation is saved.

Leading Leo places he won't go. Leo will go most anyplace if he thinks he'll be the center of attention once there. But you can't drag him anywhere that's not up to his standards. Or status.

For example, there's not much chance he'll indulge in dinner at that funky new dive you just heard about. That is, not until you tell him, "I hear Mick [meaning Jagger] always hits there when he's in town. But I see why you wouldn't want to go . . . "

If you look around and there he isn't, Leo's already downstairs hailing a cab.

Maybe Leo roars about taking you to your boring office cocktail party. Or to the opera or theater. Do you know why?

It's because at one of your professional functions, you outrank him. Leo's the date or the bit-of-fluff. Under those circumstances, there's nothing left to do but to bribe him.

Stopping Leo check-grabbing. You meet friends at a restaurant for drinks. Just drinks. They had dinner before you got there. When it's time to settle up, what does Leo do?

"My treat," Leo says, snatching the check. If Leo keeps this up, you'll be treated right into bankruptcy. Do you feel like saying, "Stop! We can't afford it," and plopping down a twenty for your share on the way out?

Don't.

When you see the waiter coming, whisper to Leo: "Honey, John's so envious of your status. Just look at the poor guy." Poor John's smirking because he's about to be treated to a free meal. "Why don't you give him a chance to feel important? Let him pick up the tab this time."

Leo will acquiesce.

Handling the Leo lecture. The Leo lecture could be about anything. For instance:

- The value of punctuality (this delivered while you barely have enough time to get where you're going)
- Paying more attention to somebody or something besides Leo (including your newborn baby or your job while you're up for promotion)
- About the right way (i.e., Leo's way) to deal with housekeepers, subordinates at work, etc.

Don't bother arguing. This will merely net you another lecture, one on disrespect.

Instead, all you have to say is: Has anyone ever told you that your eyes are as blue as the sapphires in the Crown Jewels?

Leo will sputter to a stop, blink a few times, and smile. Then she'll pout before saying: Don't you mean my eyes are *bluer?*

Did I say as blue? Smile prettily: I meant bluer.

Lecture forgotten.

It's trickier when the Leo lecture is about Leo. Let's say you've been listening to Leo's ego-rant for half an hour. Eventually she'll say, "Enough about me. What do your friends think about me?" Just lie.

The Leo Boss

In your professional life, who does lunch the most, works the least, *and* has the biggest office? Your Leo boss.

Leo is not your boss. She's your *superior.* Leo is also good at something she calls delegating, but her envious enemies call shirking. Like the Leo friend or lover, the Leo executive must be paid proper respect. Don't dress better than she does, and don't complain about how overworked you are. Any Libras who point out how unfair this is have already transferred into a position under the more passive Pisces. A Leo boss is the most unfair executive there is. It's a dictatorship. Don't forget it.

How to Handle a Leo Boss

As you may have deduced from the rest of this chapter, all Leos are bosses. Here's how to deal with the one who signs your paycheck.

Check in. Often. You're accountable to the Leo boss at all times. Leo wants to know what, how, and who you're doing. If you don't tell him, he'll make you pay. It's better to keep him informed from the beginning; it's less trouble—at least a little less trouble.

> You: I'm off to the post office. Can I do anything for you while I'm out?
>
> Leo Boss: Oh, no, not a thing, I don't want to impose. Just some limited edition Cole Porter stamps and a snack on your way back.

Tell them to hold the horseradish this time. Last time, I blew bad breath all over a client. What were you thinking of? And while you're out, you may as well pick out some lingerie for my wife's birthday. What? Oh, use your own judgment. You know I'm not one of those domineering bosses.

You: *(swallowing)* Yes sir.

Be appreciative. Remember the trinket Leo gave you for your first anniversary on the job? If it's jewelry, wear it. If it's not, refer to it. Often. And in front of other people.

You: *(at lunch with Leo and other coworkers)* I just love the Degas print you gave me. It hangs in my bedroom so it's the first thing I see when I wake up in the morning. *(Smile gratefully.)*

Leo will think, "I knew I was right to hire her. She's got great taste."

Show Leo respect. Ranks and titles mean a lot to Leo. The Lion thinks they establish his rank as your superior. Always call your Leo boss "Mr." or "Ms." Remember this fetish for rank when it comes to using first names, too. If your democratically minded Leo answers to "John," you'd better call him "Jonathan." Even if John is his real name, call him Jonathan. That's what he calls himself.

Play on Leo's pride when asking for a raise. The Leo boss can't stand anyone to think he can't afford something. That would mean he wasn't important—and that he couldn't take care of all the peasants. Try this when you want a raise:

You: Ray Cheatum of Cheatum and Snell [a rival firm] said our business was shaky. And that it would be a strain for you to give me a seven percent raise. I told him he was crazy.

Leo Boss: He sure is. Are you sure seven percent is enough?

Let Leo take center stage. Leo wants to talk. Keep your mouth shut and let her.

Later, she'll say to herself, "I just love talking to her. She's a brilliant conversationalist."

Give Leo credit for your work. You may as well give it to him. He'll take it anyway. Boss-Above-Leo calls a meeting. You're unprepared. Leo breezes into the conference room, all smiles.

> Leo: We've been working really hard on this. I told my assistant here all about it. Take it away.

Leo waves his hand at you. Everyone stares. Your palms sweat as you shuffle through your files. Then you're saved by a blast of inspiration.

> You: I think we should—I mean, here's an approach Leo boss has himself been toying with for some time. First, we . . .

It was a brilliant idea of yours. No, it was a brilliant idea of Leo's. Do you tell anybody the real story? Not if you want to keep your job.

Volunteer for menial tasks. You may as well. Leo will volunteer you anyway.

How Not to Handle a Leo Boss

Don't challenge Leo's orders. Be careful when Leo makes a suggestion (in Leo language, this is also called "giving an order" or "issuing a decree"). Maybe you disagree, but you don't want to challenge her. Good idea.

Instead, reply with phrases that preserve Leo's self-respect while keeping your options open. "I'll keep that in mind," "That's a good point," or "I've never thought of it that way" are good examples.

Don't go over Leo's head. In other words, don't mention Leo's boss. Leo doesn't want to be reminded that there is such a person.

$$\mathcal{N} \quad \mathcal{N} \quad \mathcal{N}$$

In life with Leo, remember that Leo is the star and should be treated with the respect due to someone with top billing. If you pander to Leo's ego, you can more or less get away with anything, including Leo's car, credit cards, and spouse. Just don't forget that Leo is notorious for having star-quality tantrums. You've got to admire the Leo charisma—it's mandatory.

8

Virgo, the Virgin:
Ministering to Minutiae

Out to Solve a Problem: Please write me a letter listing your problems in order of urgency. (Enclose a self-addressed stamped envelope for a reply.) I'll fix whatever isn't working in your life. Then—schedule permitting—we'll have dinner at eight and sex after our shower. You can also reach me at my Web site (see below). It's capable of improvement and is constantly under reconstruction. Pardon the mess: sawdust and dust-bytes everywhere . . . oh dear, I missed a spot.

Virgo sun:	August 24–September 23
Planetary ruler:	Mercury
Virgo Web site:	*www.penmanship/cnts*

There's a Virgo stereotype that's not worth discussing: that of the celibate and fastidious vegetarian who does nothing but correct your grammar, add footnotes to conversations, and wash your plate before you've finished eating.

While it's true some Virgos are inclined toward cleanliness and proper vegetarian diets, many are carnivorous and have never formed an intimate relationship with a broom.

The stereotype is a smoke screen created by natives of the sign Virgo to protect themselves and fool other people. Virgo is actually the object of universal lust. There's something unsullied about Virgos that makes you want to drag them to the depths of depravity and hope they'll do your laundry while they're there. While you try to do that, Virgo will lure you into helplessness.

Purity is their bait. Watch out for it.

Beware the Virgo Seduction

Before manipulating Virgo, learn how the sign seduces you and insinuates itself into your good graces. Virgo is looking for trouble. Yours. Here's how he finds it.

Beware the Virgo Intellect

Behind Virgo's serene face is a shining mind. This mind will illuminate all the problems in your life. Especially the ones you don't want to see.

Virgo was invented to create order and inject calmness into chaos. Virgo won't do anything to you she's not willing to do to herself. And Virgo will do anything, including organizing her own life. Now she wants to organize yours.

⊶ *Lesson:* If you succumb to the Virgo seduction, Virgo will organize you beyond recognition.

Beware the Virgo Helpfulness

Helpfulness is how Virgo rides the entrance ramp into your mind. It starts out innocently. Say you're in a scuffle with an ATM machine. It keeps spitting out your card and beeping at you in a menacing manner. You try again. The same thing happens. Then you hear a voice coming from somewhere behind you.

Voice: Have you tried sticking it in stripe-side-down?
You: No, I hadn't thought of that.
Voice: Let me show you.
You: *(with bemused gratitude when the screen flashes the PIN prompt)* Thank you.
Voice: I'm glad to be of help.

Suddenly, you shudder. You feel a chill go down your spine and half expect to see a black limo with tinted windows pulling up alongside you. Was it your imagination or did you hear the phrase Mafioso used when coaxing into a car those inconvenient people who will soon be wearing concrete boots: "Let's go for a ride."

➻ *Lesson:* If you let Virgo seduce you with helpfulness, you'll find your life is in danger. Of being taken over by Virgo.

Do you want to manage the Virgin? Managing others is Virgo's career. Not only does she love her job with a passion that's immoral, but she's also a 168-hour-a-week workaholic. Manipulating Virgo is also quite a task because the Virgo cleverness will spot your efforts to be cunning.

On the flip side, Virgo's compulsion to help you vaults her into performing feats you'd have to scam all the other signs into doing. Virgo revels in life's tedium: She yearns to run errands, balance bank statements, and find missing socks. Just ask. Is there a price for this helpfulness besides your soul? Yes. You'll run on Virgo's schedule. Not only are there no free lunches; there's also no free time.

Recognizing Virgo

To avoid being taken over by Virgo, learn how to recognize him before he finds you. Like Gemini, the Virgin is a communicator. Unlike chattering Gemini, whose sport is the verbal volley, Virgo's conversations have a purpose—such as telling you what to do in a polite but conversationally relentless way. You'll find Virgo:

- Soaking up or disseminating information in a library
- Earning an advanced degree at an academically impeccable university
- Brutalizing an opponent in a game of full-contact Scrabble
- Making a schedule and sticking to it
- Making a schedule and making you stick to it

Manipulation Through Communication: How to Use Verbosity on Virgo

Effective communication is essential to manipulating Virgo. Remember, Virgos are verbal and will prove it if you let them. Naturally, the sign is intrigued by verbosity.

↪ *Lesson:* Virgo might actually listen to you if you use Virgo words.

Attract Virgo with Sexy Words

The words *schedule, work, polished, detailed,* and *organized* fall into the category of sexy words to a Virgo. So knock yourself out.

Seduce Virgo Verbally

You can also get what you want from Virgo if you use certain phrases, especially ones in which you confess your ineptitude. Try saying things like the following.

You: *(squinting at your computer screen while looking con-fused)* I'm really stuck. Can you think of a better way to set up this spreadsheet? *or*

You: *(leaning over the kitchen sink)* I'm making a mess of this. Will you help me pry the spoon out of the garbage disposal?

Then whatever you're doing will be out of your hands and into Virgo's.

➻ *Lesson:* Act confused, and Virgo will volunteer to become your non-wage slave.

Communicate with Precision

➻ *Lesson:* Be precise and logical when talking to Virgo. Do it by learning new Virgo words. Virgo requires precise speech from you, but you won't get it in return. Virgo invents definitions of his own, and you won't find them in *Webster's* or *The Oxford English Dictionary*. Learn the following definitive Virgo definitions:

- *Intuition*—A confused mental state. Symptoms include belief in philosophies that cannot be proven by logic, the scientific method, or the help of a slide-rule. This thought disorder plagues artists, mystics, and other people who hold no advanced degrees in economics. *Note:* Help sufferers by teaching a course in logic.
- *Spontaneity*—An unpredictable event seized on by disorganized individuals in order to subvert scheduling. Succumbing to spontaneity can lead to chaos and a disorganized calendar and is to be avoided at all costs. *Note:* Consult your calendar frequently.
- *The Big Picture*—A slang term for "totality." A word used by those unaccustomed to precision; its purpose is to divert one

from concentrating on details. Repeated exposure to the big picture results in loss of perspective. *Note:* Avoid art galleries, cameras, and individuals with imagination.

↝ *Lesson:* These are imprecise words. Don't use them.

Virgo's Achilles' Heel: Fixing Things

The Virgin fixes things like broken alarm clocks, cracked automatic fountain-pen fillers, and warped human beings. The compulsion to fix other people's problems makes Virgo the object of interplanetary pursuit. Why submit to life's details if Virgo is there to ask:

- Did you check the oil in your car?
- Did you use the correct postage on that letter?
- Did you remember to pack an extra pair of hiking boots in your knapsack?

Some Virgos are so addicted to helping that they do it for a living. It's nice that Virgo's work is also her hobby. Take advantage of it.

Taking Shots at Virgo's Achilles' Heel
Encouraging the Helper to Help You Your Way

Virgo enthusiastically volunteers to do everything from chairing committees to making coffee. Virgo has decided these are your priorities. But you haven't. You'd like Virgo to clean out the gutters or change the radio station. Here's how to get Virgo to do what you want.

Allow Virgo to help you his way . . . at first. First, indulge Virgo by letting him do favors for you that he'd like to do, but that you don't need. For example, Virgo is convinced you should reshelf your books. You'd rather have a new filing system for your paperwork. After the Virgin has rearranged your books according to subject matter, set him to work on the filing cabinet.

→ *Lesson:* Let Virgo have his way at first; then you can have your way with him next.

Keep Virgo busy. Virgo must feel useful. Constantly. Play to it.

> You: Will you wait for the telephone repairman on Saturday while I go shopping? *and*
>
> You: Would you like to volunteer to be the bookkeeper for our neighborhood investment club?

Virgo will say yes to both.

→ *Lesson:* The Virgo idea of hell is to have an empty to-do list and a blank appointment calendar.

Complain to Virgo. Virgins are problem-solvers; they quaff complaints the way alcoholics slam down cocktails. Therefore, it's no surprise that Virgos have lots of problems. But they never have enough and are on the make for more. Share your own and those of your friends, family, and coworkers.

→ *Lesson:* Aim complaints and problems in Virgo's direction. She doesn't mind. She gets off on it.

Paralysis Through Analysis: The Problem with Virgos

You have a problem. And you can't complain to Virgo because you want to complain *about* Virgo. Why would you want to defuse such a helpful soul? Virgo has been devotedly and alarmingly helpful. And done nothing more dissolute than load forks into the dishwasher tines-down. But Virgo has started analyzing.

The Virgo analysis goes like this: Pick it to pieces, look at it from all angles, think about it, analyze it, put it back together, and start all over.

You see the problem.

This is fine if the object of Virgo's fixation is something like a malfunctioning copy machine. But it's unnerving when Virgo pulls out the dissecting tools and starts working on something animate—like you.

Once you've been analyzed by Virgo, you'll feel exposed, picked to pieces, scrutinized from all angles, criticized, turned inside-out. . . . Here's how to deal with it.

You can't just tell Virgo to stop analyzing. If you do, Virgo will launch into a theory about why you don't want to be analyzed. The best way to deal with Virgo analysis is to turn the tables on him. Try the following tactics.

Give Virgo something else to pick apart. Remember the Virgin's penchant for details, unquenchable thirst for information, and compulsion to assist. Divert Virgo by asking her to unearth a little-known and supremely boring fact that would help you.

> You: I'm tackling a tax accounting project at work. Can you research the rule concerning making estimated tax payments for next year when you can't estimate your next year's income?
>
> Virgo: Yes.

The Virgin will dive into volumes of the Internal Revenue Code, wade through the paragraphs, and swim the subsections for an answer. With luck, it'll take her a while. And you can pull yourself back together while she's doing it.

Leave your errands to Virgo. Because Virgos love to keep busy, they love to do inane things like run errands. They even like to run *your* errands. If you need to go to the hardware store to get a new lock for your garden gate, the pet supply store to get nectar for your humming bird feeder, and the office supply to get a new cartridge for your printer, delegate it to Virgo. This will keep Virgo from analyzing . . . for now, anyway.

Leave the room. Sometimes there's no escape from the analysis without escaping from Virgo. But be crafty when giving your reason for leaving. Recall the Virgo intellect and logic. Feed Virgo a logical and acceptable reason for your escape.

> You: *(consulting your day-book)* This is a very interesting discussion. Unfortunately, I have an urgent appointment.

The Vices of Virginity: The Virgo Lover

Your Virgo lover is smart, well mannered, devoted, house-trained, and sexy in a quiet way. Virgo's an earth sign, which means the sign is earthy. Sexual. No wonder everyone wants to seduce the Virgin.

Being a salacious sign, Virgo is turned on by many things. Try the following to titillate Virgo and entice him into helping you on a more intimate basis.

How to Turn On Virgo
Ask Virgo about work.

> You: Your job must be very interesting.
> Virgo: It is. I design accounts payable systems for natural gas pipeline companies. . . .

Virgo then goes into great detail about his job, his day at work, the fax machine's paper-jam—and all with an expression of rapture usually seen only on the faces of canonization candidates.

➻ *Lesson:* Asking Virgo about his work is the equivalent of a champagne and black-lingerie seduction.

Demonstrate your intelligence. Blow the dust off your diplomas. Frame your Mensa membership. If you have neither, display a few volumes of the Encyclopedia Britannica, preferably on your bedside table. Virgo will be ensnared.

➻ *Lesson:* Virgo is turned on by three-digit IQs.

Make a good impression on dates. Make a good impression when treating Virgo to a romantic evening. Virgo is no slave to Emily Post etiquette, but she does like the niceties of romance. Small things count. Like punctuality and communicating well with the waiter.

It's date night with Virgo and you'll stop at nothing to impress. True, you didn't have exact change for the parking meter. But that didn't hold things up for long; you were only seven minutes late for your dinner reservation. Later, when you tipped the waiter, you did forget the tip should've been for 15 percent of the bill before tax. But you made up for all that by having to walk only three blocks out of the way to find the car. You made a nice impression. Where's Virgo? Virgo has moved in with you. You're irresistible. You need help.

➻ *Lesson:* Virgo lovers are turned on by incompetence.

Keeping the Virgo Lover Interested

Continue your campaign of acting both intelligent and incompetent. Virgo will take care of you, the paperwork, the laundry room, the recycling, the renewal of your subscription to *Smithsonian* magazine, and the quest for superior cleaning products. Virgo will also reward you by being distressingly faithful.

You'll feel distressed in other areas, too. You've discovered a Virgo vice that threatens your peace of mind and the state of your union. What's wrong? Virgo hasn't found fault with your grammar or personal grooming. Or started conjugating irregular Latin verbs during sex. But Virgo's delirium for details has taken over.

You're drowning in the minutiae of life. You know exactly where to find your purple toothbrush and savings account deposit slips, but somehow your big picture got lost at the photo-processing lab.

It's nice that life's details are under control. But so are you. And you can't indulge in pleasure because it's not detailed and it's not on the schedule. Before committing Virgo to detail detox, try the following coping techniques:

Put "fun" in Virgo's schedule. Self-sacrificing Virgo is addicted to delayed gratification and will take anything except a vacation. You want to have fun. Your idea of fun is watching movies, or exploring art museums, or frequenting flea markets. Virgo's idea of fun is to work and keep a sharp eye on wandering trivia.

You: Let's do something amusing today. How about seeing the Bauhaus exhibit?

Virgo: I'm working. Besides, we don't have any social engagements until next Friday.

You: Haven't you noticed the new entry on the calendar? We're due at the art museum in an hour.

➻ *Lesson:* Trick Virgo into having fun by slipping amusements into a slot on the calendar.

Act incompetent. Say you're cooking dinner, and you've looped the linguini around the pot handle.

You: This is such a tangle. I can't seem to unravel the pasta.

Virgo: Yes, it's a mess.

As Virgo detangles the linguini, it should remind you.

➻ *Lesson:* Virgo salivates to correct your mistakes. Make them, and let her.

Virgo Lover Don'ts

Don't take Virgo criticism personally. Virgo's vision is especially keen when it comes to spotting flaws. Everything is capable of improvement. Especially you. Don't take it personally.

Don't disturb or disorganize Virgo's belongings. Organization is as precious to the Virgin as harmony is to a Libra or a high-yield stock portfolio is to a Capricorn. True, Virgo lovers like to fix your mistakes. But don't mess with theirs. Keep the CDs in Virgo's music collection in order. Tidy the Virgin's kitchen pantry. Arrange the laundry by color while it's still in the laundry basket. Virgo will be enthralled.

Don't alter Virgo's routine. Or environment.

Virgo will criticize you if you do certain things. Commit any of the following misdemeanors, and Virgo will send himself into a quiet snit and you around the bend:

- Don't reset the alarm clock without permission
- Don't move the milk from the refrigerator door to the top shelf
- Don't be late for meals
- Don't reset the temperature on the thermostat
- Don't analyze Virgo

Virgo is the expert analyst. When it comes to analyzing, Virgo doesn't go both ways.

The Virgo Boss

There's another Virgo myth that's not worth discussing: Virgo is so dedicated to service that she'll only work for other people. And as a result, there are few Virgo bosses. This is not only untrue, but is a rumor started by Capricorn career-snipers in quest of promotions.

Remember, Virgo's life revolves around fixing messes—unless Virgo is your boss. When Virgo engraves the title "Manager" on her office stationery, her cosmic urge to help you is snuffed out. Other bosses consider employee guidance part of their jobs. Not the Virgin.

Not only will the Virgo boss decline to fix your messes, she considers your cock-ups proof of incompetence. Although Virgo is beguiled by incompetence in lovers and friends, she'll annihilate you if you expose it at the office.

☛ *Lesson:* Exude competence at the office.

Keep Your Virgo Boss Happy

Here's how to keep your Virgo boss off your back:

Arrive at the office promptly. Prove you're a paragon of promptness by getting to the office on time. Better yet, arrive early. Not only should you get there before the morning cleaning crew, but make sure your Virgo boss knows it.

☛ *Lesson:* Punch in loudly enough for your Virgo boss to hear you.

Concentrate on details. Details count to your Virgo boss. Sometimes they're all that count.

Remind Virgo of the day's meetings.

> You: Don't forget your eight-fifteen meeting with the systems analysis manager.

Reminding Virgo of his own schedule is as unnecessary as reminding a librarian that Dostoyevsky fails to make light reading. Virgo's calendar is etched into his brain cells. But he'll remember your reminder.

☛ *Lesson:* Impress a Virgo boss by showing him you share his fervor for routine.

Make a to-do list. Write down the day's tasks in front of your Virgo boss, especially the trivial ones. Then scratch through each item as it's finished. Make sure Virgo sees you do it.

→ *Lesson:* Drafting a task list proves you're organized, which is as important to your Virgo boss as keeping a clean global environment and ordering the right-size paper clips.

Account for your time. Maybe you need to pop out of the office for some fresh air or perspective or a cigarette made from leaves grown in Jamaica.

> You: *(to your Virgo boss)* I'm going to run around the corner to see what's holding up the courier. I'll be back in ten minutes.
> Virgo Boss: No problem.

Your boss doesn't mind the detour, but remember.

→ *Lesson:* Come back in ten minutes. You might be the type who loses track of time while admiring the blossoms on the trees and the cracks in the sidewalk.

But your Virgo boss definitely isn't.

♍ ♍ ♍

Life with the Virgin can be full of seduction. It can also be filled with analyzing, slavish devotion to calendars, and more than anyone's fair share of tasks (read: chores). Virgos are well known for having a fetish for appearing modest and unassuming. Don't assume that they're easy to handle, though. When manipulating Virgo, stay organized at all costs, and don't let life toss a tidal wave over your best-laid plans. To prevent being one of those people who clutches their calendar like a shipwrecked sailor clinging to a life raft, anticipate every difficulty you can imagine, check the details, and check and double-check your appointment book. Then delegate it all to Virgo.

9

Libra, the Scales:
Frantic for Balance

Partner Desired: Balancing the scales has special requirements. On one hand, it requires a law degree from Harvard, the services of a general staff, and a spin doctor. On the other hand, you must also mesh with my idea of harmony, beauty, and perfection. On the other hand—oh, dear, I have now run out of hands and would be most grateful for yours. They must be soft of skin, polished of nail, and accomplished at juggling. Please write to me on embossed stationery and I will reply by return post.

Libra sun:	September 24–October 23
Planetary ruler:	Venus
Libra Web site:	*www.radical/middle*

Libras are the persuaders extraordinaire of the zodiac. Libra gives the appearance of being balanced. He's so pleasant, so refined, and so lovely to look at. Libras have nice smiles and beautiful voices. This is to disguise their steely determination and razor-sharp minds.

It's said in astrological circles that Aries has cornered the market on leadership. Because of their forthright manner, Rams just appear to be in charge. Aries are really the frontmen for Libras, who rule the world.

Here's how they do it and what you should be aware of.

Beware Libra's impeccable manners. It's so easy to relax around the Venus-ruled Libran. Libra always consults you politely. Chivalrously, even. Let's say you're meeting Libra for breakfast. You walk into the kitchen, and Libra greets you with a smile.

Libra: I don't know how you like your eggs.

You: *(to yourself)* How considerate.

Before you go into a soliloquy about the merits of eggs benedict versus huevos rancheros, look around you. Is Libra standing there with an egg whisk in one hand and a poacher in the other? No.

Does Libra's question mean he is making breakfast? No. You are.

Beware Libras seeking opinions.

Libra: What would you like to do today?

Oh good, you think, we get to go to the zoo instead of the theatre. Libra *seems* to be asking your opinion about what you'll do for entertainment. She's really just setting it up so that she can tell you what she wants to do.

➡ *Lesson:* When Libra approaches you with an opinion-seeking question, it's a signal that Libra has already made up her mind. It's the only occasion when this happens, so enjoy it.

Beware the Libra considerate nature. Libra will disarm you with apparent consideration, especially when doing something he knows you don't like.

Libra is doing something you agreed is against the house rules. Since you both value your sleep, you agreed there would be no loud music after 11 P.M. and no lawn mowing early on Saturday mornings.

Then one night you hear Beethoven's Ninth blasting from the stereo or the nerve-grating sound of the lawn mower at 8:00 A.M. on Sunday. Deciding Libra needs to be reminded of your agreement, you prepare for a debate.

You storm downstairs thinking about tactics and trying to decide whether to use reason or guilt or to go with your inclinations and use raw anger. There stands Libra, smiling with concern.

Libra: Is this a bad time to be making all this noise?

You reel from this consideration, so apparently at odds with Libra's actions, and are stumped. Then you find yourself muttering: "It's okay," and volunteering to hear the symphony through to the end or get more gasoline for the mower.

➻ *Lesson:* Don't take consideration for an answer.

Recognizing Libra

Would you like to be part of Libra's civilized and refined world? You can find Libra:

- Reclining on a velvet sofa and avoiding taking a stand
- Leading others with the melody of his voice and the depth of his dimples into doing what he wants
- Teetering atop of the scales of justice and jumping from one scale to the other

- In a courtroom arguing both sides of the case with passionate detachment
- In an embassy issuing diplomatic statements, demonstrating his talent for saying nothing at all with great distinction
- Deferring judgment (i.e., never making up his mind)

Libra's Achilles' Heel: A Calm and Peaceful Atmosphere

If you can be calm and keep your head in life's little emergencies, Libra will keep you around. Indefinitely.

Yes, this need for calm contradicts Libra's penchant for lively debates. Think of the symbol for Libra: the Scales. Have you ever tried to balance an old-fashioned scale? When you put weight on one side, the other side shoots up. Then when you try to even it out with weight to the other side, this side rises. If this is hard to imagine, think of a seesaw's action as it goes up and down.

Sometimes it's hard to keep score. Which side are you on? Which side is Libra on? Don't ask Libra. Just remember whose side you're on. Yours. Remember to convince Libra you're on his side. Just be prepared to switch at a moment's notice.

The Venus-ruled Libra spends life in a quest to be aggressively moderate. This back-and-forth movement is tiring to Libra and exhausting to watch. Yes, Libra is undeniably pleasant, ever so reasonable, and even-tempered. Yet when you're around her for long, you fear the knot in your stomach is growing into an ulcer and everybody knows only Virgos get ulcers. There must be something wrong with you, you think. Before you accuse your mother of forging the date on your birth certificate, think.

The Libra Lecture

Libras like to hold forth, but their lectures are more like discussions. They enjoy back-chat. Natives of the sign of Libra are great thinkers. Libra thinks mostly about arguing, a sport she calls "lively debate." You're more likely to call it cruel and unusual punishment.

To Libra, arguing is the highest form of entertainment and her favorite amusement. Unless you get off on debates, don't push the arguing/balancing button.

Your Libra lover has the ability to be charming and blunt at the same time. When you find yourself falling for Libra charm, go off and repeat Libra's remarks into a tape recorder and see if you'd fall for it if you said it yourself.

The Libra Lightshow

Libra just *appears* to be light. Before you decide that light banter would not only go over his head but through it as well, think again. Lightness is just a disguise Libra uses to throw you off-guard when preparing to do a psychological takedown.

The Pseudo-Suggestion

You've had a lovely dinner with Libra. Then your lovely lover makes a suggestion.

> Libra: Would you like to come and talk to me while I do the dishes?

It seems awkward to just stand there and let your lover do all the work, so you start scrubbing the pots and pans, cleaning the sink, and tidying up generally while Libra loads the dishwasher but doesn't start it yet. You're pleased, and judging by Libra's usual sweet smile, she seems pleased, too.

As you sit in front of the television with an after-dinner cognac, Libra glances into the kitchen and sighs. "Shall I run the dishwasher? Maybe I'll wait. The kitchen isn't as clean as I'd like it." Then Libra smiles again and gives you a squeeze.

You think Libra is apologizing. Think again. She's chastising.

Yes, you.

Seducing the Seductive Libra

As the happy recipients of seduction, Libras are custom-made. They love to be in relationships, and they love to be romanced. Use the traditional tactics of muted lighting, soft music, and lovely meals. You might throw in an extra or two, like a massage or a love note. It never hurts to lay in a supply of candles to set the atmosphere. Little things mean a lot to Libra. Libra will always be charmingly thankful for the nice things you do. You'll be thankful you romanced them, too. Libras can be wonderful to have around if you're in the market for romance. If you're in the market for wildness and unpredictability, then you're out of luck with Libra.

Libra loves the idea of a partnership. Very early in the relationship you can say things that forecast a future. For instance, say something like this: "I just love being with you. You're good at things I'm not good at, and vice versa. We complement each other beautifully. We make a great couple, don't you think?"

If you're used to an independent type like Sagittarius or Aquarius or a slippery soul-mate like Pisces, a comment like that would send them bolting out the door. Not Libra. He loves being in relationships. You'll love it, too, if you keep the following "Don't" in mind.

Libra Don'ts

In a relationship with such an agreeable sign as Libra, there is only one don't. It's a big one, though. *Don't get thrown by Libra debates.*

You're a particularly sensitive soul who picks up on other people's needs and responds to them instinctively; so, of course, you expect others to do the same. Remember Libra loves to engage in lively debates (i.e., arguments). Your Libra lover isn't being insensitive; she's just being Libra. You feel. Libra thinks. And she thinks mostly about arguing, a mental sport she prefers to call "energetic conversation."

Of course your Libra lover is charming. Libra is probably also good looking. This is the cosmos's way of disguising the fact that all Libras are lawyers at heart, no matter what they do for a living. And what do lawyers do? They see two sides to every question and argue both with equal conviction. So does your Libra lover. When you say, "Yes," Libra automatically says, "No."

How do you win an argument with Libra? It's tricky. You can't even walk away from one, because Libra will pick up where you left off the night before. The only way to deal with a Libra argument is to do this:

> You: I'm sorry. You're right.

Then when Libra's trying to figure out whether you're sorry about what you said or whether you're merely sorry that she's right, you can go off and restore your mental equilibrium.

The Libra Boss

You love working for your Libra boss. How can you help it? The atmosphere is calm. The Libra boss knows that comfortable workers are productive workers. If you're used to the austerity of the all-business atmosphere of a Capricorn boss, you're in for a surprise.

Your workspace is tastefully decorated with soothing colors. Libra will encourage you to be comfortable. If you're convinced your productivity is linked to playing classical music, Libra will clear a place for a portable stereo system. If you're inspired by artwork, Libra will be happy to ask maintenance to hang a reproduction of a lovely Ansel Adams landscape.

The atmosphere is equally soothing. In a dispute with your fellow workers, your boss is fair—judicial, even. Libra is always logical and fair in dealing with office politics. Is it any wonder that positions under Libra are highly sought after? Yes, people are dying to work for your Libra boss. There's a snag, though.

You have a beautiful office, pleasant workplace, and a smiling and understanding boss who has no complaints. The closest Libra ever got to rebuking you was the time he said, "I've been looking at the department income statement. I hope the revenue numbers plump up next quarter."

"I agree," you said.

You're thinking of revenue, in the abstract. Libra is thinking about your sales figures, in particular.

If the numbers aren't up by 25 percent, it will show up on your performance evaluation. If you're still with the firm, that is.

The overriding problem with working for a Libra boss is you don't know where you stand. On eggshells, probably. This conversation about revenue targets was a warning.

➼ *Lesson:* Read between the lines with your Libra boss, or you'll be reading hints on how to rev up your resume for a new job.

Libra bosses are nature's politicians and are Teflon executives extraordinaire. When things go bad, Libra still looks good. If something goes wrong at the office, Libra will don the coat of compromise, which is a dirty word to most of the other astrological signs. This is a clever Libra loophole. Your Libra boss excels at creating detours—and just took one. Unfortunately, you didn't, so don't blame the boss.

➥ *Lesson:* In professional life with the Venus-ruled Libra, take the blame. You can always give it back later.

♎ ♎ ♎

Libras possess undeniable charm, a pleasant demeanor, graciousness, and a host of other irritating attributes. Above all, Libra is diplomatic. With that soft smile and undiluted charm, Libra is almost always able to get his or her way. To get your way with Libra, keep your voice down and your head down. In the manipulation game, Libra is one of the pros. Do you get the impression Libra is a sniper in cheerleader's clothing? Then you're right.

10
Scorpio, the Scorpion:
Crimes Against Chastity

Psychosexual Services Available. I'm every sin you'll ever commit. I want to spend all night psychoanalyzing you, leatherwear supplied. I'll keep you so busy, you'll never notice the locks on the doors and the video cameras in the bedroom. Watch out: I don't take prisoners.

Scorpio sun:	October 24–November 22
Planetary ruler:	Pluto
Scorpio Web site:	Unlisted

ote on Guerrilla Warfare. Scorpio is the master of single-minded subtle manipulation, double bluffs, and invisible probing. To protect himself, he wants to keep you in the dark. Not just because you can't see him that way, but because he lives in the dark. In fact, the only time a Scorpio will turn on the lights is to have sex.

Know what you're up against.

Keep Your Eyes Open

Beware the Scorpio Lie

➥ *Lesson:* A Scorpio will lie about anything she considers none of your business. Like her name, sex, and phone number. If you ever find out somebody lied about her birth date, you'll know she's a Scorpio. Some take this self-protection to extremes. Like Andy Warhol.

Only an astrological imbecile would've thought Warhol was a Leo. Just look at the guy.

- He wore black.
- He lied about his birth date.
- He made dirty movies.
- Somebody shot him.

Beware the Scorpio Disguise

➥ *Lesson:* Scorpio is never what he appears on the surface. Or just below the surface. Never ever.

If he reads the *Wall Street Journal* on the commuter train, he reads *Domination Digest* before he goes to bed. If he wears overalls and sports a buzz cut, at home he reads Shakespearean sonnets and watches PBS. If he chants mantras and rattles tambourines for the

Krishnas, he actively supports the abolition of free speech.

If he ignores you, he wants to screw you.

So you want to take charge of Scorpio. This is tricky, risky even, because Scorpio's so good at taking charge of everyone else. He's been crafty and cunning from the time he wore diapers, so he knows what move you'll make even before you make it. Maybe even before you think it. The chances of beating him at the manipulation game are low, and the cost of failure is high. If you get caught, that is. And you will.

Imagine this: You've got an itch for your Scorpio friend's lover. "I'll ask her out," you say. "The worst she can do is turn me down." She turns you down. So what?

So this: Scorp always thought you were out to get him. Now he knows. What'll happen? Don't ask. Just hand him a riding crop, drop your jockey shorts, and bend over.

Detecting Scorpio

Would you like to cavort with a Scorpio? You have to find her first. You're most likely to run into her:

- In a bar
- Checking out the talent on a nude beach
- Behind the throne (See the shadow cast by the president of your company? It's not his own. It's Scorpio's.)

Perhaps you don't have a taste for booze, coasts, or castles. You can still find the Pluto-ruled Scorpio any place there's a mystery to be solved or a deviance to be indulged. But it takes a talent for detection. First of all, look for someone intense and magnetic. You think you can spot him with no problem? Spot the Scorpio in the following list.

- The woman spilling out of her low-cut, spangled sweater at the corner deli
- The stockbroker-type guy who's flipping through *Psychology Today* on the elevator
- The woman who's reading a volume of poetry while waiting for the subway

They're all Scorpios. See? Subtle.

Defending Yourself Against Scorpio

Before trying to manage the master, learn how to defend yourself. Whether your Scorpio is a lover, a boss, or a friend, remember this: The best defense is the only defense. Here are some common Scorpio tricks:

The invisible wire. Scorpio will trip you up by getting you to reveal yourself. He'll take the opposite stance on an issue he believes in just to see if you'll agree with it.

A conservatively dressed Scorpio will say, "I advocate the death penalty for an unrenewed dog license." Oh joy! you think, another conservative. So you slip him the secret fascist handshake and proudly display your nifty white designer sheets. But he doesn't seem nearly as excited as you'd expected. Why?

He's a flaming liberal. A paid-up member of the ACLU. And he just tricked you into exposing your politics.

The strip-search. Your new Scorpio girlfriend may be a fluffy bunny of a girl. Or your Scorpio friend is so kind, you expect him to become the next pope. But these are a couple of the sneakier disguises.

All Plutonians are really little district attorneys or FBI agents.

And every one is a strip-search expert. If you're late getting home, he thinks you stopped to screw somebody else. If you mention him to your boss, he thinks you're plotting to get him fired. Whatever you've done—or he thinks you've done, or thinks you may be thinking of doing—be prepared for an interrogation.

The last confession. "Tell me about it," she says. That velvety voice. That understanding expression.

Feel the urge to confide? Don't.

That urge has led many to spill secrets to Scorpio. What would she blackmail you for? Nothing so obvious as money. Favors, more likely. Introductions to people in power.

But blackmail isn't the only reason she wants to hear your secrets. Knowing your secrets is insurance against future Scorpio felonies—a "Get Out of Jail Free" card. How can you spill that she pads expenses at work when she knows you faxed the Yellow Pages to India at the Christmas party?

It's worse when Scorp knows your secrets but doesn't do anything at all. Every now and then she'll flip through the secrets filed away in her lock box of a brain. And she'll let you watch just for the thrill of seeing you squirm and keeping you in line.

What Not to Do with a Scorpio

When dealing with Scorpio, it's unwise to do any of the following:

Do not flatter Scorpio. Or try to bribe Scorpio. "Don't flatter?" you say. "Don't bribe?" Go ahead. Try it.

Your Scorp husband won't take the hint about buying a new car. So you cook his favorite dinner and wear your naughtiest lingerie. Over a candle-lit dinner, you say, "You really are a peach of a husband."

In the morning, you feel smug about the sweaty night's work you put in after the lights went out. When you wake up, the garage is still empty. So is your bed. Don't worry, he hasn't run off to Bermuda. He's in the kitchen steaming open your mail.

↦ *Lesson:* Flatter a Scorpio, and he'll think you're plotting against him.

Do not bullshit Scorpio. If you're feeling the seduction of social bullshit, do the party circuit with a Gemini. With Scorpio, you'd better be yourself, even if you're afraid she won't like what she sees. Especially if you're afraid she won't like what she sees.

Scorpio: *(confirming a date)* Are we still on for the play tonight?

It sounded fun a week ago. But now all you want to do is stay home and pick fleas off your dog. But you're afraid to offend. So what do you say?

> You: It sounded fun a week ago, but all I feel like doing tonight is picking fleas off my dog.

↦ *Lesson:* Scorpio was born with a bullshit detector, so don't try to be smooth.

Don't tell Scorpio your secret weapon is astrology.

↦ *Lesson:* Scorpio assumes astrology was invented just so other people could figure out how to snatch his power and invade his privacy.

He may not believe in astrology, but he'll get nervous if he thinks you're using it to learn how to handle him. A nervous Scorpio is an unsafe Scorpio. Practice this:

Scorpio: Let's say a person's born in November. What sign does that make him?
You: *Uh.* Virgo?

Scorpio's Achilles' Heel: Sex

It's the only thing about himself a Scorpio can't hide. You won't have to surreptitiously sneak around looking through Scorpio's bedroom drawers to discover her sexual secrets. She'll broadcast them loud and clear—in stereo. Scorpio lives for sex. Radiates sex. Is sex. And if you want to bond tightly with Scorpio, get used to buying condoms by the case.

Dangerous Liaisons: The Scorpio Lover

What's in this for you? Sex. As much as you can handle. But beware. Scorpio has refined sex as the ultimate experience in weaponry.

Power is also what's in it for you. In your career, in politics, around the house, anywhere the Scorpion wriggles his eight little legs. Scorpio has it, and if you get in good with him, he'll share. The price is total domination. Ever heard of Doctor Faustus?

Luring the Scorpio Lover

➼ *Lesson:* The universal Scorpio aphrodisiacs are power and mystery.

To attract her, you'd better have plenty of both. But be careful how you show that power and mystery. Something that impresses the other signs will probably piss off a Scorpio.

Scorpio Turn-Offs

Posers. The Plutonian dislikes phonies. After all, if you're a fake, you must have something to hide. Scorpio is suspicious of and bored by the electronic props of power—like cell phones, PDAs, pagers. Leave your poser-phone at home.

Invasions of privacy. Scorpio makes a religion out of privacy.

Remember that the next time you're tempted to snoop through her mail, eavesdrop on a phone call, or look under her bed.

You might guess from all this she detests crowds. How can a person be private in a crowd? If you see her in the middle of one, you can be sure she's on her way somewhere secluded. Intimate even. Leos have a problem here: In close quarters, there's no room for the Leo entourage. Send the entourage on vacation.

Flightiness. Scorpio can't stand surprises. If he can't predict something, it means he can't control it. A flighty or unpredictable person will send him running.

If you're a typical Aquarius, you'd better pretend you're a Taurus.

Handling a Scorpio Once You've Got One

Never fool around sexually. Why would you do that anyway? There *are* reasons to flirt with carnal exploration. Maybe you're sick of multiple orgasms. Or tired of never getting to be on top. Go ahead and experiment. But make the lover a good one—it could be the last you'll ever have.

Be secretive. It's hard to keep secrets from Sherlock. Try, though. He'll get bored if he thinks he's figured you out. Make up a few secrets to keep him interested. Try locking up your address book, and then watch him turn into an amateur safe-cracker.

Play sex games. Things getting too routine? Try this.

> You: *(calling your Scorpio girlfriend at work)* Meet me at the Chelsea Hotel in two hours. Bring the economy-sized box of condoms, some electrical tape, and a video camera.

Don't do this often, or you'll find yourself manacled to a Scorpio without a job.

The Scorpio Boss

They're out to get your Scorpio boss. You don't think so? Your Scorpio boss thinks so. She knows so. At night she even dreams about it. During the day, she tweaks the antennae that warn her of plots in the workplace and pulsations in office politics. She's the one who thought up new conspiracies for episodes of *The X-Files*.

Imagine she walks in on a gossiping crowd in the copy room. Suddenly everybody shuts up. Don't bother telling her you stopped talking just because you were telling a risqué joke and didn't want her to hear it. You were talking about her, and she knows it.

If she looks into a mirror, it's not to see if her hem's straight. It's to warn her who's sneaking up behind her. And how many sharp knives they're carrying.

The keyword with Scorpio is *control*. Your Scorpio boss controls you—body, soul, and bank account. But you'd better control yourself, too. She hates whiners and other people who lose their shit in public. If you see a Scorpio who comes unstrung, what you really see is someone pretending to be a Scorpio.

You're in a real bind with your Pluto-ruled boss. If you don't do your job well, she'll think you're lame. If you do it too well, she'll think you're out to get her job. While you're working for her, never ever challenge her authority. And forget maneuvering her into giving you a raise. One day, you'll find yourself either promoted or fired.

Don't talk about your boss behind her back. Don't go over her head. Don't tell anybody her plans. You'll get caught; her spies are everywhere.

The Plutonian wants to know everything that goes on at the office. Like what brand of soap the janitorial staff uses and how much you cheat on your taxes. But she frowns on gossip. Maybe you'd like to be one of her spies. Say you've just tripped back from a gossipy, two-martini lunch.

Scorpio Boss: Did you have a nice lunch? How is old George? (George is your coworker and Scorp's employee.)

You: He's fine. More than fine. He ought to be, with that invitation to the vice president's weekend place. (This is an honor Scorp hasn't been given yet.)

Scorp: Oh?

You: Yeah, for next weekend. I'm not supposed to say anything, though. Think something's up there?

Scorp: *(smiling a chilly smile)* Let's go over that sales report now, shall we?

You: *(to yourself)* George has had it now.

Wrong. *You've* had it now.

→ *Lesson:* You'd better not gossip. Scorpio's radar is the envy of every dolphin's. Unless she asks, she doesn't need yours.

Besides, you just told somebody's secret. Now Scorp knows she can't trust you.

→ *Lesson:* Be loyal. If you aren't, Scorp will do what he's famous for—he'll get back at you.

Astrology says Scorpios are ruthless and determined. But you don't believe it. Your Scorpio boss is so quiet, so together, so laid back. Not explosive or scary at all. You've been to his house. There were no missals to the Black Mass, no coffin for him to climb into after a long night.

You're feeling cocky, so you push him. You do one of the things you should never do to a Scorpio: You tell his secrets.

You won't have to wait long before something like this happens:

You: *(to yourself)* I just told a secretary about my boss Steve's failed first marriage that nobody knows about. He didn't say a word.

Feeling relieved, you decide he must be a Pisces after all. Or a Sagittarius who forgot he was married before. You know you've done the unforgivable. So what does Scorpio Steve do?

He forgives you.

Like the innocent you are, you breathe easily. A month passes. Six months, a year. Suddenly, you find yourself:

- Turned down for a sure-thing promotion
- With your legs squeezed together outside the executive washroom holding a key that no longer fits
- Unable to reach Steve because he's in a meeting, or on another phone line, or away from his desk, or—you get the idea

You: *(to yourself again, because nobody else in the office will talk to you either)* I'm confused and a little hurt. What does Scorp Steve think he's doing?

Stop talking to yourself, and buy a newspaper. Tear through it until you find the "Career Opportunities" listing—you're going to need it.

That, and the astrology section.

♏ ♏ ♏

When you run into a Scorpio, he seems like everyone else. It isn't surprising that Scorpio doesn't seem sinister; he just seems sexy. After this encounter, you leave the office, aiming for the corner deli where you'll pick up your evening meal. Instead, you find yourself buying black lingerie at Victoria's Secret. Later, when you should be putting in hours on your budget report for work, you wonder how you might profit from twisting the sheets with an old lover. Psychologists call this an unhealthy sex fixation. Astrologers call it a Scorpio Encounter. Don't be surprised if you're tempted to commit crimes against chastity.

11
Sagittarius, the Archer: Gambling with Immortality

Traveling Companion Wanted: STOP To all independent and philosophical companions STOP I'll treat you to a trip to Monte Carlo, but you'll have to bankroll it until I break the bank again STOP You'll like me. I'm wise and blunt, but please don't respond using one of those stupid preprinted postcards like Virgo did. I mean, I like Virgos and everything but [please] STOP All correspondence forwarded.

Sag sun:	November 23–December 21
Planetary ruler:	Jupiter
Sag Web site:	*www.passing/port*

f a Sagittarius has bounded into your life, get ready to go on lots of trips. Update your passport, check out prices on long-term parking at the airport, and learn how to communicate from a distance. Not only will you be invited to travel to exotic places, your mind will be tripping on the qualities of honesty, optimism, and luck.

Sagittarians are delightful traveling companions. If anybody can take you to the depths of frankness and cheerfulness and bring you back untainted by the experience, it's the Archer.

Sagittarian honesty, optimism, and luck are legendary. So is Sag directness, which means he is not a manipulator. And so, he is oblivious to your attempts to manipulate him. Lucky you.

⇥ *Lesson:* Don't look for hidden meanings with up-front Sagittarius. The Archer is either there or not. To read anything else into him is a waste of energy you could put into a tangle with a Pisces or Scorpio, whose mind games take up all their cerebral disk space.

Know Sagittarius's Secret Weapon

Before you manipulate Sagittarius, be aware of his secret weapon: amiability. Everyone loves Sag. How can you help it? Sag is fun and likable, and he will show you the positive side of life whether you want to see it or not.

Be aware of the ways Sag uses this appeal to draw you in and keep you around under the direst circumstances. Here are some of Sag's ploys.

Optimism

If you look for the roots of the inspirational book movement and positive-thinking seminars, you'll find Sagittarius at fault. For blind faith and optimism, Sag has no peers.

When everyone else is saying you'll never get that promotion, never qualify for that mortgage, never find a lover who can toss together deals as well as salads, Sag says: "You will." No wonder it feels good to be around him.

→ *Lesson:* It's impossible to feel gloomy, depressed, realistic, or practical around a Sag. This is his biggest weapon and there's no defense against it.

Cheerfulness

If Sag can't cheer you up with jokes, philosophies, or stories of magnificent luck, she'll take you to a bar at which she has frequent flyer status with the bartender.

Sag is the only sign that likes to tell good-luck stories. This is foreign to a Capricorn, for example, who regularly entertains gloomy thoughts. To Sag, entertaining the bad is just a waste of energy and a good night out.

Sagittarius is the zodiac's proof of the light side: Every cloud has a silver lining. It's darkest before the dawn. There's always another credit card company, and being divorced three times is really no big deal.

You'll put up with anything to be in a Sagittarian's company. You'd be crazy not to.

There's a problem, though. You'd like to have a quiet word with Sag on your own. But no, there's a big crowd around the Archer. Her agent is there, her producer, her bookie, her debt collectors, and her many other admirers who want to get her alone just as much as you do.

→ *Lesson:* Forget exclusivity: it's not happening here.

Sagittarius's Achilles' Heel: An Open Mind

There's a deep reason for Sag's taste for terminals and pressurized cabins. Sagittarian airport-lust is a symptom of the Archer's need for freedom and wide experience. Travel is one legal way to satisfy it. Besides, travel broadens the mind, and there's nothing Sag likes more than a broad mind.

Sag's penchant for being places other than where you are poses a problem: It's hard to manipulate someone who's not there. Yes, he's often taxiing down a runway or hailing a cab. But when Sag does occupy the same time zone with you, he's still traveling. Mentally. This mental openness strips him of camouflage and provides you with a nice target. Psychologically. Read on to find out how to push your luck and pull the trigger.

Tracking and Tricking Sagittarius

Sagittarius is so gregarious that you'll notice her immediately. Besides brightening people's days at airports and on cruise ships, Sagittarius is:

- In Las Vegas, Monte Carlo, or any place with multiple casinos
- At the bank, trying to convert dollars into pesos, pounds, or Euros
- At the bank, persuading the loan officer to give him one more month

All this travel and experience has made Sag knowledgeable and philosophical and overdrawn. There's nothing academic about the Sagittarius approach to life. Sag learns from experience and therefore wants to have as many experiences as possible.

To Sag, this is a justifiable need to solve the riddle of existence by going where she likes, whenever possible. To you, it may seem like excessive unavailability and a reluctance to commit to anything more confining than a seat in Economy.

So you'll have to trick her into living real life. Your way.

Tricking Sagittarius into Real Life

There are a couple of obstacles to tricking Sag into doing what you want. The first problem is that Sag finds the details of life boring. The best way to manipulate your Sagittarian friend, lover, or employer is to scam him into thinking real life is as fun as a trip. For example, conceal the tedium of running errands with the aroma of travel:

- Trick Sag into thinking grocery shopping is like traveling by sending him out to buy ethnic food
- Tempt Sag into dealing with the laundry by asking him to drop by the dry cleaners on the way to the airport
- Pander to Sag's need for freedom of movement by suggesting he e-mail the next quarter's budget

The second obstacle to getting Sag to participate in his own life is that philosophical mind. Sag has such a global philosophy, it distracts him from life's details. It's a trait that interferes with a smooth daily life. Yours.

You must be alert to Sag's philosophies in order to get him down to earth and under your control.

The Sagittarius Philosophy of Life. There's always a moral to the story, a lesson to be learned, and another one just around the corner. Don't get the idea you're indispensable.

Sagittarius Philosophy of Religion. The sign is famous for its religious side, but this aspect of the sign's personality moves in mysterious ways. Yes, the Archer has found all the answers and unlocked the mysteries of religion, either orthodox or obscure. But Sagittarius's real religion is sharing information, so he often takes the word on the road to sinners in casinos and exotic dance clubs.

Sagittarius Philosophy of Natural Selection. As far as sex goes, natural selection is one of Sag's philosophies. It means that if somebody's there, well, naturally they're selected.

Beware Sagittarian Frankness

For all the Sag happy-go-luckiness, she's someone to be reckoned with. Honesty is her most formidable weapon, the use of which you should discourage.

Sag is no con artist. When she wants more time, more interim financing, more chances, she'll never try to blackjack you. She'll ask you straight out. But don't follow her lead. You may end up with more honesty than you're ready for.

➥ *Lesson:* Never ask Sag to tell you the truth, unless you're prepared to hear it.

Beware Sagittarian Honesty

You're going to the beach with Sag and are proud of the new resort-wear you bought with the money you should've invested in paying your phone bill.

> You: *(to your Sag girlfriend, as you show off your new Speedo)* How do I look?

As you bask in the compliments, you suddenly realize Sag has given you none. Instead, she's trying to explain what she really meant when she said you were fat.

Sag: What I mean is it's great to see somebody who's an individual. Not as individual as my ex, but somebody who doesn't just follow what everyone else is doing, and somebody with courage. I mean I can see how brave you are to go out in a bathing suit. I mean, it really is a compliment.

➺ *Lesson:* Don't ask Sag's opinion unless you can take it.

Beware Sagittarian Indiscretion

Naturally, since Sagittarius is so blunt and matter-of-fact, he has a sketchy idea of what information should be keep secret or what should be shared with other people. Just to be on the safe side, though, don't tell him any secrets. It can be tempting, especially when you're stressed out or sad.

Let's say there are problems in your marriage. Your kindly Sag friend notices you look glum and wants to cheer you up. So he invites you out for a drink.

Sag: You look like you've lost your best friend or something. (Sag thinks about how many friends he has and decides to share.)

You're attached to your misery and want to keep it to yourself. Then you get a bit careless after he's ordered you your fourth Manhattan.

You: It looks like I might lose my best friend. My marriage is in trouble.

Sag: *(appalled at your bad fortune)* Don't be sad; it's no big loss. I mean, everybody knows your soon-to-be-ex never stopped screwing around in case things didn't work out.

Then Sag notices your jaw has dropped and hastens to reassure you.

Sag: I mean *I* never did. I just heard everyone else has. Hey, don't worry. I've been married three times and I don't even remember my ex's name anymore. Hey! bartender. Another round, my friend here needs it. I mean, wouldn't you if your marriage was on the rocks?

Too late you remember.

→ *Lesson:* If you want to keep your personal life personal, don't tell Sag any secrets.

Beware the Backhanded Compliment

You feel gloomy. You missed your connecting flight because of a pilot's strike. The Archer decides to improve your outlook and your day. Cheerfulness and sincere compliments are bound to make you feel better. The Archer's arsenal includes both.

After brightening your day by telling you how geographically sophisticated you are, your Sagittarius coworker explains what he really meant when he said you were stupid:

Sag: What I mean is, I can see why you didn't know Latvia's in Europe, mostly because you spent so much time memorizing the state capitals. It's cool that you know all that, but you really should've been looking at a globe or at least into a mirror; that's a disastrous haircut. I mean, it's great to see somebody who doesn't care what they look l—

→ *Lesson:* Don't expect to feel better after a Sagittarian compliment. When it comes to giving the backhand, Sagittarius shares center court with the first seed at Wimbledon.

The Frequent Flyer: The Sagittarius Lover

Your prospects are good with a Sagittarius lover. If you're out for fun, intellectually stimulating conversation, and a three-digit long-distance phone bill. If you hope to announce a joint checking account in the future, your prospects aren't as good.

↦ *Lesson:* If you're looking for long-term, seek another sign.

And unfortunately for monogamy, Sagittarius's wanderlust also extends to her love life. But try to be optimistic: so maybe Sagittarius strays. So what? The Archer will be back. Ultimately, variety can be as boring as anything else.

Sagittarius Turn-Ons

Feel complimented if you've lured Sag. It means you're attractive, you're intelligent, you're there. Sag is into broad experience, which means he's open to new places and people. This is good for you because it's easy to attract him. It's irksome in the next phase of the relationship, though. Because he's open to new places and people and it's easy to attract him. For now, the best way to get what you want from Sag is to do the following:

Be positive.

↦ *Lesson:* If you're the victim of a gloomy disposition, hide it behind a few platitudes, such as: it's darkest before the dawn, tomorrow is another day, there's always a package tour available. This will protect you from the Sagittarius pep talk. And you may start believing it yourself.

Tell the truth.

↦ *Lesson:* If you have an uneasy relationship with the truth, go with another sign.

With Sag, always be honest. The Archer's devotion to the truth is very strong. So strong, she feels obliged to share it with everyone, regardless of the consequences as well as the dictates of common sense and good manners.

Be generous. Because of his own generosity, Sagittarius doesn't understand the concept of tightfistedness. If you decline to sign a check or slide the plastic, Sag will try his luck somewhere else.

Sag is optimistic. He'll have plenty of cash, even when teetering between two financial extremes. Sag shares with his many friends, acquaintances, and people he hasn't met yet.

↝ *Lesson:* Sag is generous whether he's won the lottery or just checked out of the hospital for the terminally short of cash.

Keeping the Sagittarius Lover Interested

↝ *Lesson:* A Sagittarius lover will have fun with you for as long as fun is all you want to have.

Sag is optimistic enough to give commitment a whirl—temporarily. But to expect Sag to settle down to a life of home cooking and sex on alternate Thursdays is just not realistic.

Travel light emotionally. Think of this relationship as a trip. Imagine you're traveling to New York with Sag. Sag has never experienced curbside luggage check and would think you're strange if you carry two bags. Wouldn't you develop a talent for packing a carryon bag?

So, check your emotional baggage, too. Send it one-way to Burma.

↝ *Lesson:* The best way to keep Sag nearby is to keep your emotional distance and encourage him to keep his.

What Not to Do with Sagittarius

One of the Archer's delightful traits is she rarely holds grudges. There are few things that offend her for long.

So there is only one "don't" in this relationship. And it's for your protection.

Don't take sex for an answer.

You've just been on a joint vacation with Sag and are preparing to return to your respective time zones. You're about to board your flight. Sag is about to board a different flight. You've walked Sag to her seat on the plane.

> You: I can reschedule my flight. How about it? (You mean you'd like to extend your layover for a week or so.)

Sag thinks you mean: "How about setting up housekeeping?"

The Archer gives you a deep, loving look. And leads you to the lavatory. Before you have a chance to read which federal laws you'll violate if you unhook the smoke detector, Sagittarius answers you with sex.

> You: *(to yourself later, when you're misty-eyed with the memory of your temporary farewell)* Of course we're a couple. Sag always tells it like it is.

Don't clear your closet or even your calendar for next weekend. Think. Where are you? On a plane going home. Where is Sag? On another plane flying in a different direction.

Do you still think commitments are sealed by the imprint on your ass of the "Call Flight Attendant" button? Now that's optimistic.

The Sagittarius Boss

There's a problem with Sagittarius bosses. They're never there. Your Sag boss is just as unavailable as your Sag friend or lover. But it will be less frustrating, because your emotional or romantic sensibilities aren't at stake—just your professional sanity.

Look at it philosophically. The absence of your Sagittarius boss is one reason she's fun to work for. There's little formality around the office. If you have a problem, you can go directly to Sagittarius (as soon as she gets back to the office).

Not only will she listen, she'll have an ingenious solution to your difficulties. There's little competitiveness and no paranoia about you trying to snatch her job. And she delegates with ease. She trusts you, of course.

You'll have a nice expense account, and your boss won't nitpick your expense report. You can just round it off to the nearest hundred, and leave the rest to the Virgos in accounting.

You don't have to account for your time by the quarter-hour. Sag knows not every hour is billable. She'll understand if you take a day or two off because of jet lag. And won't dock your pay if your flight was late. Sag also knows a lot of business is done out of the high-rise and after hours. Like on golf courses, in theaters, at conventions. And if you want a raise, all you have to do is ask.

You decide to ask Sagittarius boss just that. You're prepared. Sag isn't.

> You: I've been with the company a year now, and my perfor-
> mance evaluations have been good—
> Sag: You're right. You deserve a raise. How much do you want—
> (The phone rings.) It's that call I've been waiting for from
> Frankfurt. Let's finish this later.

You're happy now and start planning a new vacation to celebrate. The next day, you go to seal the deal with Sagittarius. Your boss's office policy may be open door, but there's no boss in the office.

No, she's not in Frankfurt. She's in Grand Cayman. No, that was day before yesterday. Today Sag is in Kentucky, closing a deal that happened to come together on the day of the derby.

Meanwhile, the phone's ringing. The fax machine's beeping. The in-box is filling. Your trusting Sagittarius boss left you in charge. So, take care of things.

⟡ *Lesson:* To function in your job, you'd better be able to work independently.

Learn to Communicate from a Distance

Just because your Sag boss is out of the office doesn't mean he doesn't want to know what's going on. Check your voice mail and e-mail often for updates and instructions.

Handle All Financial Matters

Left to herself, Sag would have the department on a credit line that would strain the Federal Reserve and give premature heart disease to the Virgos in accounting. Be good with figures. If you're not, take a budgeting refresher course.

Take Your Work on the Road

Since your Sagittarius boss does, he can't possibly object.

Be Detail-Oriented

Your Jupiter-ruled boss isn't. Sag's mind is on higher things, like how to get another extension on her tax return. So she can be shadowy on details. Take care of tedious tasks like scheduling meetings, directing the paperwork flow, and refreshing the stock of office supplies.

Do the Talking

A Sag boss is a great communicator, but unfortunately he can be as amusingly tactless as your Sagittarius friends. To make your boss look good and remind him to follow up on that raise, act as a translator.

Otherwise, Sag might forget his boss's name. As he once forgot yours.

> Sag: What do you think about that, Serge?
> You: My name's George.
> Sag: Right. Do you think the Masai of Kenya should abandon their warrior spirits to be safari guides for bored jet-setters? Do you, Serge?
> You: George.
> Sag: That's what I said. What do you think? Can I call you Sarge?

You finally give up. Some things are more important than correct names: like future job titles.

> You: It's Serge.

✗ ✗ ✗

Sagittarius is a high flyer and an endless propagator of optimism. Sag is also a gambler. One of the things Sag gambles on is you keeping your good will through all his conversational bumblings. Sag is used to being forgiven for tactlessness—why don't you surprise him and keep your forgiveness to yourself?

12

Capricorn, the Goat: A Fugitive from Faddishness

I've arrived—Have you? I've reached the top and now that I'm here, I find the view impressive but the atmosphere a trifle thin. Please write if you meet the following qualifications: executive or entrepreneur, well or self-made, responsible, and cultured. You must be conversant with operatic repertoire and never confuse *Don Giovanni* with one of the Long Island Giovannis.

       Capricorn sun: December 22–January 20
    Planetary ruler: Saturn
Capricorn Web site: *www.montblanc/usr*

L ife is a business, and what's a successful business without effective manipulation? To Capricorn, it's part of the civilized but cut-throat world of commerce. He's the protagonist. You're the antagonist. It's war without visible bloodshed, strategy without emotional heat. Don't worry about the consequences if he discovers your treachery. It's part of the game. Capricorn's rules of business and, therefore, of life are as follows:

First, you get to know your opponent.
Next, you respect him.
Then you kill him.

⟿ *Lesson:* Learn Capricorn's tactics. Play him at his own game and beat him. And don't be afraid to lose. If you put up an impressive fight, the Goat will spare your life. Then he'll offer you a job.

Defending Yourself Against Capricorn

The Goat has many weapons. When manipulating him, be familiar with his arsenal so you can defend yourself. But mainly, so you can use his weapons against him.

Capricorn's artillery includes patience and the element of surprise. He also has ruthless knowledge of his own motivations, as well as familiarity with his bank balance and how many zeros it'll take to bump it into the billions. Be on guard against and *au fait* with other Capricorn ploys, too.

Beware Capricorns Bearing Lunch

All that you've heard about Capricorn self-centeredness is untrue. Capricorns share rides to work, meals at four-star restaurants, and kitchen implements such as skewers. Not only does Capricorn share, she's glad to do favors. In fact, big favors are the Goat's favorite kind. They guarantee big returns.

→ *Lesson:* If Capricorn does you a favor, do one in return.

Beware the Civilized Hostile Takeover

A hostile takeover is a move in which a powerful entity takes control of a vulnerable one against the latter's will. That's not the Saturn-ruled Capricorn's style. Takeover, yes; hostile, no—if it were hostile, it would hardly be civilized.

Capricorn is always stately and dignified and even more so when doing something devious. What would Capricorn want to take over? It could be your favorite pet, your spouse, or two feet of your property line. Whatever it is, it adds to her security. It's nothing personal, so don't get bent out of shape.

→ *Lesson:* When Capricorn uses premeditated suavity, watch your back.

You decide that learning Capricorn's manipulation game is easy. That all you have to do is don corporate wear, sleep with the *Wall Street Journal*, and breathe in rhythm to changes in the Dow Jones. Think again.

You've misread the object of Capricorn's game. It's probably professional. But it's just as likely to be social or sexual. Whatever his goal, Capricorn wants to make it to the top; and when Cap says "top," he means the peak of the financial mountain. The Goat thinks money is sexy. He thinks if you're rich, everyone will want to screw you. Screw him first.

Recognizing Capricorn

You'll discover Capricorn anywhere there are mountains to climb, dominions to conquer, or culture to consume. For example, she could be:

- Climbing the corporate ladder
- Running an empire
- At the symphony, reprimanding rude people who chatter through the opening bars

Why the social and corporate climb? Capricorn knows it's lonely at the top, but it's lonelier at the bottom and not quite as comfortable. Whatever Cap is doing or however she's doing it, remember she's on the way up.

➤ *Lesson:* Capricorn knows where she's going. Either get out of the way or help her get there.

Capricorn's Achilles' Heel: Fear of Poverty

Capricorn's ambition is armor against poverty. There's security in the material rewards of ambition, and status is tangible proof of safety. This hunger for status and its impressive trappings makes Capricorn the curator of culture. It also makes him vulnerable and easier to trap.

➤ *Lesson:* If you impress Capricorn, you can manipulate him.

How to Impress Capricorn

Capricorn is a fugitive from the latest fad and has other endearing traits such as patience. But she has no patience with people who file their taxes after April 15 or don't know which fork to use at gala luncheons. If your Capricorn is a friend, a lover, or boss, try the following:

Act Dignified

Capricorn is dignified at all times and expects you to be the same. Losing your couth or dropping your decorum will earn you no points.

If you don't believe it, commit misdemeanors against manners. Use your salad fork with the entrée. Drink red wine with the fish course. Dip your savoir-faire into the vichyssoise. Then watch Cap lose his cool—later, in private.

Get Cultured

To Cap, the word *culture* doesn't exist just to be preceded by the word *pop*. Culture can be found in places like museums, art galleries, libraries, historical buildings, and cemeteries. Visit those places.

Cultivate Literacy

Here are a couple of ideas:

Speak properly. Flush the slang and study grammar books as if your pension depends on it. Capricorn will lose patience if you deprave and corrupt the English language by slipping into the vernacular, misplacing your "to whoms," or abusing your contractions.

Get acquainted with the literary classics. Renew your library card and use it. Capricorn respects people who can read. Know your Shakespeare or at least be on a first-name basis with *Julius Caesar, The Merchant of Venice, Richard the III*. And don't cheat by using Cliffs Notes.

Acquire Artistic Knowledge

View a van Gogh. Take a CD-Rom tour around the National Portrait Gallery. Capricorn will be impressed. It's slander to say Capricorn is so traditional she's actually artistically calcified. Capricorn loves art and is especially fascinated by the color of currency.

➵ *Lesson:* Acquire a refined taste in art. Just because a painting hangs in the Whitney and is lewd or incomprehensible doesn't mean it's art.

Capricorn Don'ts

Single-mindedness is the secret to the Goat's enviable ruthlessness. And it's another way to manipulate him. Snatch Cap's own weapons of focus and patience and use them against him by not doing the following:

Don't expect spontaneity. If you want someone who's short on long-term planning, you're in the wrong slice of the zodiac.

Don't be hasty. Would you like the Goat to loan you her space in the parking garage, screw the cap back onto the soy sauce, or let you use the blow dryer? Keep a sharp eye out for the right timing. Watch. Wait.

Then pounce when Capricorn is in the middle of a business deal. That's when she becomes so focused that she loses all perspective and most of her peripheral vision. Pull into her parking place when she's not looking; then for grins, replace her name with your own on the "Reserved For" sign.

Don't put obstacles in Capricorn's way. To Capricorn, obstacles were put in this world to be climbed over. Don't assume you can divert him by tossing barriers in his path. Don't distract him with complaints about the leaky roof when he's in the middle of a meeting. Don't page him at the opera while he's entertaining clients from Japan.

➵ *Lesson:* Putting barriers in front of Capricorn is like rolling a boulder onto his path—it's hard work, it's useless, and you'll have nothing to show for it except rock-burn on your hands. How tacky.

The Onslaught of Honorable Intentions: The Capricorn Lover

Your Capricorn lover is elegant and graceful. She drops nothing but names. If you're into honorable intentions, you've found the right mate in Capricorn. If you prefer kinky sex or wild romantic encounters, you're better off with Leo or Aquarius.

Congratulations for capturing the Goat's interest. Capricorn is enticed by refinement and depth. Let the other signs fall for the allure of trendy wardrobes, artificially induced tans, and seemingly sophisticated but intellectually bankrupt conversation.

Capricorn has high standards and expects the same of you as she does of friends or employees. Such as dependability, refinement, and accomplishment. This is not to say she's untouched by the sparkle of romance—because she's not—it's just that those other things are more important.

➻ *Lesson:* Capricorn is turned off by shallowness. So let's see what turns her on.

Capricorn Turn-Ons

Authenticity. If you think Capricorn is sizing you up, it's just because he is.

Remember, the Goat doesn't like fakery or superficiality. Capricorn is not seduced by the shallowness of mere physical charms, like your height or leg length. Mainly because he's gazing deeply into the core of your authentic being and lusting after your accomplishments, contacts, and social standing.

➻ *Lesson:* Capricorn won't etch your name in the family Bible if you aren't up to the job and his standards.

Courtship. Prepare for the onslaught of honorable intentions. This means formal dates, discreet inquiries into your taste in furniture, and subtle displays of Capricorn's personal real estate. It doesn't take a CEO to twig to the end goal. It's marriage or a committed relationship.

Now, Cap is not above a one-night stand. But if you submit, you'll slip from your candidacy for a permanent position. Relationships are an investment in the future, and what future is there in a one-night stand?

Lesson: To Capricorn, love is a serious business.

Keeping Capricorn Interested

Capricorn is so committed to commitment, keeping her interested isn't usually a problem. Getting rid of her is. Until you want to do that, here's the best way to get what you want.

Dress well. Remember, you're one of Capricorn's assets. If you don't look good, he looks bad. When shopping for clothes, patronize a posh boutique. Whatever you do, don't pay resale. Trot out your impressive duds.

> You: *(displaying your outfit)* This is what I'll wear to the Rotary Club banquet on Saturday.
>
> Capricorn: *(frowning)* That's what you *were* going to wear to the banquet.

Capricorn is unimpressed by your black rubber trousers and their price tag. He's also positively appalled by your idea of haute couture.

Lesson: Dress appropriately and tastefully for the occasion.

What Not to Do with Capricorn

Yes, Capricorn runs your relationship the same way she manages her sole proprietorship. Meaning, she takes work to the office, along with almost everything else. But there's one facet of her personality she never takes to the office: depression. Don't worry about it. With the gloomy Goat, it's natural. Don't do the following, either.

Don't be optimistic. The Goat is proof of the power of negative thinking. Avoid overt positivism. It will only entrench negativity and bring on nightmarish visions of the day he mislaid his Mont Blanc.

What's Capricorn worried about? It could be the weakening of the dollar, shudders in the NASDAQ, the loose wheel bearing on your car, or the fact that at your last dinner party he let avariciousness get the better of his good table manners. Whatever Cap might be worried about, you want to corkscrew him out of his easy chair and into fresh air and sunshine. If left alone, he will tend to stew in the juice of his own melancholy. Appeal to Capricorn's practical side by extolling the virtues of exercise. Besides, you want to roller-skate around the neighborhood.

The only way to seduce him into it is to persuade him it's to his advantage.

> You: *(dangling skates in front of Cap)* Come on, let's surf the pavement. It'll be fun.

Capricorn frowns. You've reminded him that if something's fun, it must be wrong.

> You: Oh, well. I thought you'd like to come. I heard the mayor takes a stroll around here this time of day.

⇝ *Lesson:* Tell Capricorn it will advance his career if he surrenders to fun.

Don't Expect Levity

The Goat is at a party, wearing a silly hat and an inane smile while tossing confetti with the other guests. Don't let this display fool you. Capricorn is always steeped to the horns in serious purpose.

She may seem to be partying, but watch closely. Is Capricorn really drinking her third gin and tonic? Or is that bubbling beverage just club soda in a rocks glass? Can you honestly say she looks like she's having fun? Think about it. Maybe the guest list includes a potential client.

➾ *Lesson:* Once you divine Cap's reason for being there, you'll realize that for her celebrations are serious business.

Don't Tell Capricorn to Do His Duty

Capricorn is always happy to do his duty. It's not possible to persuade him to enjoy anything else. Other don'ts include:

- Don't belittle his accomplishments
- Don't be tacky
- Don't consume conspicuously
- Don't expect indiscriminate complimenting
- Don't tell the Goat to lighten up

He can't.

The Capricorn Boss

Capricorn was born to be boss. Or is he merely your immediate superior? He just seems to be. Maybe Capricorn's not the chairman of the board. Flip through the corporate minutes and city records and you'll find that Cap owns the chairman, the board, and the office building. And if he doesn't already, he will. Remember that the next time you're tempted to dismiss the importance of being earnest.

Job stability is a serious threat in professional life with the Goat. Do your job, and you'll have a job to do. Permanently. Proper form is important, and so is the traditional chain of command. Capricorn put the structure in corporate structure. This means formality rules at the office. Use it to your advantage and to encourage promotions.

Appeal to Capricorn Traditionalism

Use old-fashioned types of communication and equipment. Capricorn likes letters. Or memos. Manila folders. Yellow legal pads. Fountain pens. It's okay to use modern equipment occasionally, but only if it's efficient. Cap is traditional, but that doesn't mean she'll turn up her nose at computers, electric typewriters, telephones, motorcars, and so on.

⇢ *Lesson:* Capricorn will embrace modern technology, but that doesn't mean she'll go to bed with it.

Reveal Your Ambition

Do you want more challenging projects? Do you want to deal with the general public more often? Do you want to hobnob with upper-echelon executives who can secure your promotion?

⇢ *Lesson:* Flash your aspirations. Capricorn knows there's no such thing as a lateral move, and he'll respect your ambition.

Get to the Office First

Getting to the office before your Capricorn boss arrives is not an easy feat to accomplish. She sleeps there.

Approach Capricorn Through Proper Channels

Was your former boss a Sagittarius? Did proper channels mean popping into his office and asking if you could use his hole punch? This hasn't prepared you for Capricorn.

Communicate with your Capricorn boss the old-fashioned way. Have your secretary talk to his secretary's personal assistant's intern.

Follow this up with a written request for his time. Capricorn will respond, also through proper channels. As you might guess, it takes time to navigate all these channels.

↣ *Lesson:* Plan ahead when you need your Capricorn boss's input.

Submit Detailed, Correct Expense Reports

Capricorn keeps a sharp eye on the pennies, especially those belonging to shareholders and others who live for the bottom line. Sort through your receipts and staple them to your expense report.

↣ *Lesson:* Capricorn is impressed by financial organization and thoroughness. Don't forget it.

Also don't forget to heed the following:

• Don't exceed the budget
• Don't leave work in your cubicle
• Don't bring personal problems to the office

Having trouble with your lover? Lost your dog? Divorced your spouse? Keep it out of the high-rise and tell a friend instead.

↣ *Lesson:* In Capricorn's book, emotional displays are déclassé.

♑ ♑ ♑

Capricorn is the prototype corporate climber and quite an executive manipulator on her own. Compete with the Goat by doing a little businesslike manipulating of your own. Zero in on one of her pet subjects: etiquette. If anyone knows the proper table manners to bring to a gala luncheon, it's Capricorn. The Goat is so refined and so sure-footed; she really knows what's important. Undermine Capricorn's assurance by whispering radical notions in her ear. "You're refined.

You're sure-footed. You know what's important. What if loosening up your idea of good taste is just as important as knowing which wine to serve with the fish course? Do you know you can embrace culture and kitsch?" If you're persuasive enough, Capricorn will spend some time deciding between attending the opera or going shopping for pink flamingos to adorn the front yard instead. Then you can throw her off base. And if it doesn't work either way, it's fun to watch.

13

Aquarius, the Water Bearer: Fettered to Freedom

New Age/High-Tech: I'm channeling my energy into finding someone with great computer equipment. Send me an e-mail if you'd like to help with my experiment on the freedom of orbiting. When we meet, bring your laptop and the latest in radical scientific/intergalactic thought. *Note:* My mind is subject to change without notice.

Aquarius sun:	January 21–February 19
Planetary ruler:	Uranus
Aquarius Web site:	*www.www*

Launched into a relationship with an Aquarius? Happy landing. Aquarius is a high-tech New Ager and arbiter of all that's fashionably deviant. Quirky, brilliant, and an outer-limits eccentric, Aquarius is a combination of 1960s prototype and diehard futurist who believes in a clean environment, interracial/interplanetary tolerance, and if you can't do it with a computer—then why bother.

Aquarius is such a tech-fetishist, she'll never mistake Windows XP for a new band or CDs for something you deposit in a bank. Some people say Aquarians are quirky. Others say they're from another planet.

If anything attracts the Uranus-ruled Aquarian, it's eccentricity. To capture her attention:

Emphasize your eccentricities. The Uranian has a fascination with and high tolerance for off-beam behavior. If you eat peanut butter and jelly sandwiches for breakfast, scrub the toilet at three o'clock in the morning, or live in a commune for the certifiably inventive, Aquarius won't question your sanity. Aquarius can't say you're odd. And they won't, unless you love working your nine-to-nine office job.

➡ *Lesson:* Reveal your radical behavior.

Disguise your conventional tendencies. Do you have a salaried job, a home in the suburbs, and a penchant for shopping in strip centers? Hide it. Hide your surprise at Aquarius's radical ideas, too. The Aquarian brand of avant-garde is hard to take if you're conservative. Traditionalists think all it takes to make a psych ward is an empty room and the right kind of Aquarians. If that's what you think, don't hold back.

➡ *Lesson:* Tell Aquarius he's crazy. He gets off on it.

What to Expect from Unpredictable Aquarius
Manipulating Aquarius is an interesting experiment. The sign is not

only eccentric, but unpredictable as well. But whether Aquarius is your boss, friend, or lover, there are still a few things you can expect.

Expect Equal Treatment

Aquarius may be Mensa material, but can't understand why people behave differently in different relationships.

→ Lesson: Whether you're a boss, a lover, or a friend, the Water Bearer will treat you the same, which is quite noble and supremely irritating of him. Remember, Aquarius confuses lovers with friends, friends with lovers, and bosses with friends.

Expect the Unexpected

Aquarius is unpredictable. When you want to stretch out on a blanket and make love in the light of the full moon, Aquarius says, "Sure." Then he talks about comets. When you want guidance on a project at work, Aquarius says "Sure," and then excuses himself because his Bunsen is burning. When you invite the Water Bearer to a dinner party, he says, "Sure." Then he actually shows up.

→ Lesson: With Aquarius, expect the unexpected.

Expect Eccentric Speech

Communicating with Aquarius is a unique experience. The conversation is hard to follow, and not just because of Aquarius's sizzling intellect. Rather it's because Aquarius thinks trains of thought were made to be derailed.

→ Lesson: Aquarians jump from one subject to another. Or from one paragraph to another. And leave out the connecting links. Or never finish a senten—

Remember, with Aquarius, it's never a straight line between points *A* and *B*.

Recognizing the Typical Aquarian

You have to recognize Aquarius before you can manipulate her. Aquarian unpredictability can drive you wild. This unpredictability extends to her persona and can be confusing when trying to sleuth out a Water Bearer. Aquarians are always different. From each other as well as everyone else.

↠ *Lesson:* Be observant and be aware when scoping out the Uranian.

Beware the Overtly Eccentric Scientist Guise

This Aquarian threads neckties through his belt loops to hold up his trousers and forgets basic things like where he lives. He ventures out of the lab to find gizmos to fuel the time machine he's inventing to take him back to Woodstock I.

He's the stereotypic absentminded professor. This doesn't mean his mind is missing; he just misplaced it. It might be at the health-food store, the gadget shop, or the seminar on how to impregnate mathematicians with a little personality.

↠ *Lesson:* Avoid him or he'll touch you for a development grant.

Beware the Apparently Conforming but Closet-Eccentric Uranian

This Aquarian appears to be as conventional as a stockbroker and almost as exciting. The disguise helps her sneak up on you in inventive ways. This type thinks the *X-Files* are documentaries and the world will end in a month.

Notice the briefcase-carrying woman who's scanning the magazine racks at the grocery store? Yes, the one who's wearing the regulation 1½-inch heel pumps and waist-strangling pantyhose. You'd swear she never thought of anything more radical than a profit and loss statement. Look more closely.

Her earrings are made of titanium and are shaped like flying saucers. She's not flipping through *Fortune* magazine, but a Sci-Fi/New Age journal that tells you how to download meatloaf recipes directly from the cosmic Web without using a modem.

➥ *Lesson:* Aquarius is the one who looks like everyone else. And isn't. Other than that, recognizing them is a free-for-all. You'll know one when you encounter one.

What Not to Expect from Rebellious Aquarius

Aquarians are so independent and rebellious, you'd expect the word *don't* to be as objectionable as the word *authority*. But remember the sign is unpredictable, and there are things you shouldn't expect from your Aquarian friends, lovers, or bosses.

Don't expect to control Aquarius. Aquarius is uncontrollable; and though he has integrated into our world, he's not been domesticated yet. Any attempts to make him over or take him over will blow up in your face.

➥ *Lesson:* Aquarian tolerance hits a meltdown around control freaks.

Don't expect order and method. If you think things should be done a certain way, at a certain time, and only when it's a certain temperature, readjust your attitude.

➥ *Lesson:* What looks like chaos to you is business as usual to Aquarius.

Don't expect practicality. Aquarius turns her laser-sharp mind to important things like agitating for world peace, inventing the perpetual motion machine, and unraveling the intricacies of cold fusion. However, she still hasn't grasped that you shouldn't wash dark colors with light colors and that you must first fill a car with gasoline before you can drive it.

↦ *Lesson:* To Aquarius, quantum leaps are no problem. Only life's infinitesimal steps are beyond imagining.

Aquarius's Achilles' Heel: Rebelliousness

Everything about the Uranian is different, including his lifestyle, ideologies, politics, diet, and brain structure. He rebels against a traditional life. Being unconventional is the core of his identity and the only constant in his life. It's also the method by which he's constantly able to be manipulated. He's so busy reacting that he rarely thinks of subterfuge or power ploys. Aquarius is a genius, so, of course, he understands the concept of manipulation—in theory. But not in practice. So you'll get to practice on Aquarius.

The Universal Aquarius Manipulation Tactic

Aquarius is unwilling to bend to orders, but you can still get what you want from her. The following example applies to a relationship with any Uranian, whether professional, romantic, or friendly. The basics remain the same.

Use Reverse Psychology

There's a microchip implant in the Aquarian brain that says: "If someone tells you to do *A*, do *Z* instead." So, Aquarius is an easy mark for reverse psychology. This is the astrological sign Freud had in mind when he invented the technique. Use the following as a template for getting your way with all Aquarians: Tell Aquarius he cannot, should not, had better not, there's a law against it, so he should never _____. (Fill in the blank with whatever you want him to do.)

Then he'll do it.

There's a catch, though—you have to catch the mentally elusive Aquarian first. You'll probably catch Aquarius acting like an absent-minded professor. He's perfectly capable of calculated thought, though. Before trying to manipulate him, remember: *Aquarius has a brain. Don't let him use it.*

Maybe there's a boring task on your agenda that Aquarius doesn't want to do. Then he'll beam up and hide behind his inventive mind. It's a personal protest against authority and control. Yours.

Let's say you've been nagging your Aquarian lover for weeks about installing an automatic sprinkler system in the front yard. Aquarius is perfectly willing to pour time into reversing entropy, but he feigns airheadedness when you mention sprinklers.

Try saying the following: "Under no circumstances are you to pull up my Bermuda grass and put in those insidious sprinkler heads. I'd just trip over them while taking the dog out at night. Besides," you add calculatingly, "as of today, it's against the zoning laws."

By morning, you'll find that Aquarius has spent all night tumbling your turf and defying the city planners. And you have a beautiful dewy lawn to prove it.

➡ *Lesson:* If you want Aquarius to do something, tell him he mustn't. And if you can dredge up any bureaucratic body to back up your orders, the more likely Aquarius is to defy you both.

The Velcro Relationship: The Aquarius Lover

Nowhere is Aquarian tolerance and open-mindedness more evident than in a love relationship. There's no possessiveness. No jealous tantrums if you want to explore other romantic options while enjoying a relationship with Aquarius. If this sounds too good to be true, it isn't—if you're into freedom. It is too good to be true if your idea of a relationship means regular dates and exclusive access to your lover's free time and toothbrush.

Rethink Your Definition of Love

To have a successful love relationship with Aquarius, you have to rethink your idea of love. Like everything else about the Uranian, Aquarius's concept of love is different and quite handy (for Aquarius). Think of the substances that hold relationships together. Symbolically. These materials fall into various categories:

- Cement (Taurus)
- Electrical tape (Scorpio)
- Velcro (Aquarius)

The Aquarian romance is a Velcro relationship. Aquarius wants the freedom to peel it on and off when it's convenient (for Aquarius). But inconvenient or not (to you), there is one thing you shouldn't do: *Don't be possessive.*

Remember Aquarius chafes at control and needs stimulation from many sources. Aquarius is also open-minded and believes in freedom. Add these things together and mix them with love. Then you get a situation that interferes with your domestic routine, because you can't make up your bed when there are all those people lying in it.

➻ *Lesson:* Don't expect your Aquarian love affair to be pure and unadulterated.

Keeping the Water Bearer Around

Now that you're in a relationship with Aquarius, prepare for an out-of-body experience. Aquarians are notable for being everywhere except the place they should be at the moment. To keep Aquarius around requires all the charm, subtlety, and low cunning of a Libra.

You must appeal to Aquarius's unconventionality. And satisfy his need for freedom. You can keep him endlessly intrigued, therefore eternally interested, if you pay attention to his turn-ons:

Give Aquarius space. The Uranian needs plenty of room. Give it to him. You're at home with your Aquarius lover.

Aquarius: You know how much I value our relationship. But you're in the same room with me again. . . .

You're gazing into the mirror and admiring your new haircut, so you didn't really notice he was there.

You: Am I bothering you? I'll give you some space by going to visit Fred.

You leave to go watch TV with your friend Fred. Just as you've settled in with a snack and the latest *Frasier* rerun, there's a knock at the door. It's Aquarius.

Aquarius: I thought I'd join you guys. Where's the popcorn?

➼ *Lesson:* Give the Aquarius lover space. Then he won't use it.

Embrace the Aquarian version of carnality. Such a cerebral sign must be above earthly pleasures of the body. Non-carnal. You'll often find Aquarius in bed demonstrating this quality with someone other than you.

➼ *Lesson:* Use reverse psychology when you catch Aquarius in the act of being non-carnal.

You've strolled into the bedroom and what you see makes your pulse race: Aquarius is in bed twisting the sheets with another lover. Take a deep breath and deliberately ignore your stroke-inducing high blood pressure.

You: *(with a tolerant smile)* I'm glad to see you're living up to our polygamy agreement. Under no circumstances are you to be monogamous. It undermines the biological imperative of reproduction. And it goes against all our beliefs to confine ourselves to just one person.

Aquarius: You're right.

Suddenly, the Water Bearer disentangles from the distraction in the bed. He gets up, grabs you, and kisses you—and then he does something really radical.

Like makes a commitment.

The Aquarius Boss

There are many advantages to working with an Aquarian boss. You'll be treated like an equal. She'll never think your professional purpose is just to send e-mails or channel paperwork in the proper direction. Your boss will never reprimand you if you play computer games. And she won't monitor the length of your phone calls.

You'll have the highest-tech equipment in the company: the fastest Internet connection, the most RAM, the sleekest laptop, and the most tolerant boss in the company.

Just don't call Aquarius that. The *B* word is anathema to an Aquarius. The word *boss* brings flashbacks of scuffles with authority and shows Aquarius she's become the very thing she once rebelled against.

➤ *Lesson:* If you call your Aquarian boss a boss, she might remember she has the freedom to fire you.

Call Your Boss a Team Leader

That's how he thinks of himself. And you're accountable not just to the Uranian but to the group as well—meaning your fellow employees and the top-floor executives whom you know exist but have never actually seen.

Be Independent
If you couldn't think for yourself, Aquarius wouldn't have hired you. Keep thinking for yourself. In her mind, you're being paid to give your opinions.

Be Computer Literate
Do all your projects on computer. The only paper on your desk should be ready for manual-feed or refreshing the upper tray. For leisure reading, subscribe to magazines that prophesy that the sexy new computer line for next year has already been obsolete for the past six months.

Play on Aquarius's Sense of Community
Your Aquarius boss is concerned about you and the other team members. She wants to do something that's good for liberty but bad for your job security. You want to discourage her.

Aquarius: *(at a meeting)* I've given thought to this. Contracting out is the only answer. Then none of you will be confined to this building and have to punch a time clock.

You know freelancing would work. Unfortunately, there's no way to make sure you'll be the person who gets the work. You decide absolute freedom is great, but there are limits.

You: How inventive of you. Let's think about it first. Then we can have another meeting.
Aquarius: Good idea.

You speak Aquarius's language. Now she remembers why she hired you. She might even start remembering your name.

> You: *(to your boss, six weeks later)* Are we still on for the next meeting?
> Aquarius: Yes.

Aquarius hasn't noticed that nothing has been resolved. Or figured out that you've used these meetings as a decoy. She's also forgotten what you were meeting about in the first place.

Job saved.

Ask for Instructions Rarely

Only ask for instructions if you must do something Aquarius might object to. Remember, an Aquarius boss expects you to think for yourself. But he's unpredictable, too. Yes, he's tolerant, but you're not sure exactly what he's tolerant about at the moment. So it's wise to cover your ass when you're about to do something you suspect he thinks is evil—like the profligate use of paper, for instance.

Contrary to his opinion, you can't get information to your clients using just the computer or the infamous Aquarian telepathy. You have to print something out on actual paper, affix actual postage to the envelope, and leave it to the vagaries of the U.S. postal service.

> You: Would you like this information double-spaced or single-spaced?
> Aquarius: Well, that is a problem. Think about global warming. The sacrifice of the rain forests just for the sake of McDonald's and Crane Paper Company.
> You: What if I—
> Aquarius: *(who's not listening)* If you print it out, you'll have to mail

it. And I'm not sure I like the stand the government takes on postal strikes. Not to mention the fact they won't give Timothy Leary his own postage stamp. That is a problem.

Be responsible to the forests of the earth and stop listening before Aquarius bores a hole in the ozone layer.

↦ *Lesson:* Now that you've covered your ass, decide for yourself. After all, we're all individuals.

〰 〰 〰

Politics are an Aquarian specialty. The Water Bearer can usually be found circulating petitions, picketing the razing of the rain forests, or lobbying on behalf of the oppressed. Yes, maybe Aquarius is an expert, but it's fairly easy to get Aquarius to do something. All you have to do is tell Aquarius she's not allowed to do whatever it is on your agenda. Then, of course, Aquarius will do it. Another way is to trot out a hated Aquarian foe: authority. Step back, though. As soon as you bring up the *A* word, you'll see the underbelly of agitating: smear campaigns, false advertising, and double-dealing. Prove your political savvy by stepping aside. Will Aquarius be upset with you? She would be if she remembered. But she's already turned her attention to more important things, like circulating petitions, the rain forests, lobbying on behalf of the oppressed, and so on. Lucky you.

14

Pisces, the Fish:
Searching for Synchronicity

Are you my karma?: I want to hook up with someone who'll trade a transcendental experience for a roof. Please make room for my art/poetry/movie collections and any strays I might encounter. Call if you can take charge while I indulge in diminished responsibility from behind my rose-colored Ray-Bans. Try to take charge of me, though, and you'll find I was Houdini in a previous life.

Pisces sun:	February 20–March 20
Planetary ruler:	Neptune
Pisces Web site:	*www.reality/is/overrated*

Beware Pisces' Elusiveness

Pisces is an artist. A dreamer. The empathetic, sympathetic, spellbinding soul who wants to serve and save the world. Pisces is an elusive poet who searches for salvation and escape through art. Pisces will also escape from you. This is Pisces' manipulation specialty. Know whom you're dealing with.

Beware Pisces' Anonymity

Pisces hides behind anonymity and likes to operate from behind the scenes. Pisces doesn't want to be shy. She'd rather be invisible. And even if her body is there, her mind has gone on a walkabout.

➥ *Lesson:* Don't try to get a grip on the Pisces identity. Grasp gently.

Beware Pisces' Shape-Shifting

Not only does Pisces change physical location, he changes shape and color, like a chameleon. And he can even change the surrounding atmosphere.

Pisces disappears. Is the Fish composing an epic poem behind your oak tree? Sketching your portrait from under the hammock? Or is Pisces in another time and place?

Pisces reappears, and the thought of prosody and iambic pentameter floats into your mind. Gradually, the image of your lawn blurs and transforms into the sight of a gondola floating through the water of a canal. You are now in Venice, Italy, and it's the nineteenth century. . . . There you sit, relaxing in a sidewalk café. You're sharing your second flagon of wine with Lord Byron and listening to him recite stanzas from *Childe Harolde*. Pisces is also there, pale and alone as he steps from the gondola. The Fish wears a poet's smock and a tortured soul, is doomed and will die of tuberculosis by the side of the canal.

No, he just looks that way. Rub your eyes and look around you. It's not the nineteenth century. You're mowing your lawn, not sipping wine by the light of the moon. Pisces is wearing a T-shirt, not a smock. The Fish is not doomed. Will not die of tuberculosis. He has the constitution of a sailor on shore leave—and the same motivations.

The master of illusion has concealed his true self. He has shown you what he wants you to see. He has melded with the surroundings or created new ones. Pisces has transcended time and place and taken you with him.

↬ *Lesson:* Don't be taken for a ride by Pisces' shape-shifting.

When manipulating Pisces, remember the sign's planetary ruler is Neptune. Neptune's symbol is a trident, which is an elegant word for "pitchfork." Pisces will poke you with the pitchfork at unexpected times.

"That can't be," you say. "Pisces is so kind. She always gives to charity and seldom kicks the cat."

The next time you're pricked by those tines, you'll whip around, expecting to catch a stinging Scorpio. Or a charging Ram. But nobody's there. Then you turn back around and there's your Pisces, a gentle expression on her face and a halo around her head.

↬ *Lesson:* Pisces can sneak up behind you while staring you in the face.

And while you're at it, hide the cat.

The Art of Manipulating Pisces

When you dabble in the fine art of manipulating Pisces, you're dangling your toes in frothy seas. There's nothing shallow about the Neptunian. Unfortunately. To manipulate your Pisces friend, boss, or lover, get into the right mind-set.

Get Unreal

Throw out your pretensions to practicality. Pisces has an uneasy relationship with reality. Restrict his reading of newspapers. Don't let him open his W-2 form.

↪ *Lesson:* Don't confront Pisces with real life or he'll just sit by quietly and hope it goes away.

Become Creative

The Fish's perceptions reflect through the prism of her creativity. Since she's creative, she'll relate to you better if you are, too. Exchange your toolbox for tubes of paint and a palette. Throw out your map of the United States and consult a map of the solar system.

↪ *Lesson:* Become creative, and you'll create a better relationship with Pisces.

Think in a Nonlinear Way

Embrace realities outside the visible realm. Pisces is in tune with the infinite. The Fish can explain the mysteries of Stonehenge, guide you to King Arthur's grave in Camelot, and tell you exactly what the Knights of the Round Table did with Excalibur. Just don't expect him to remember where the car's parked.

↪ *Lesson:* When you're with Pisces, think of life in the abstract.

Look under the Surface

Life is complicated. The Pisces personality is even more complicated. You'll find empathy. You'll find compassion. You'll find twelve different points of view on every issue. Don't expect to find easy answers.

↪ *Lesson:* To Pisces, there's no black or white. Only a grayer shade of gray.

How to Recognize Pisces

Pisces is so cunning with her camouflage; it's essential you learn how to recognize her. Remember, unless she's reveling in creativity or compassion, Pisces is always more comfortable behind the scenes. You'll find Pisces:

- At a social-service center, giving or receiving counseling
- At the symphony, conducting an orchestra or a clandestine love affair
- At an art gallery, psychic fair, or any place artistic, sensitive, or enlightened people congregate

The mystical nature of Pisces leads him to loiter in unusual places, such as shops that sell crystals, incense, and illusion. It's easy to lump the Neptunian into the New Ager category. Pisces gets kicks hiding anywhere, even in a category. But Pisces is really New Age with a mystical difference. And while all Pisceans are New Agers, not all New Agers are Pisceans.

Pick the Pisces

You're standing in the parking lot of an incense shop, doing reconnaissance on enlightened beings. You've spotted a couple of New Agers wearing tie-dyed T-shirts. One of them's probably a Pisces. But she might be an Aquarius. To discover which is which, ask a fashion question:

You: Is that a real tie-dyed shirt? Or is it silk-screened tie-dye?

New Ager One: *(eager to make a new friend)* It's silk-screened, the newest in graphic T-shirt decorating technology. But I'm inventing a laundry detergent that tie-dyes without tying or dying. I think I left a fire going in the lab. See you.

New Ager Two: *(warily, as if you expect a firm answer)* This? Oh, it's tie-dyed. No, it's silk-screened. (She's getting misty-eyed.) I used to wear tie-dyes I made myself, until I saw a guy selling these shirts out of the back of his truck. His wife is sick and his kids are orphans, so I bought a few T-shirts. Well, a dozen or so. I can show you where his truck is . . .

New Ager Number One is an Aquarius. Number Two is a Pisces. Not so hard to tell apart after all.

↪ *Lesson:* Pisces can't conceal her sympathetic nature. Take advantage of it.

 Pisces' Achilles' Heel: Sympathy
Pisces needs to be needed and is cosmically incapable of resisting appeals for help. That's why so many Fish are in caring professions such as medicine, social work, and roadside maintenance. Ask Pisces to help. He will.

Communicating with Pisces

Communicating with Pisces is perplexing. He doesn't communicate in the normal verbal/written/spoken way. Pisces suffers from a superstition of syntax and would rather communicate telepathically. He feels his way through life using a combination of intuition and sonar.

Pisces is tuned into conversational frequencies the rest of us have no access to. Thank God. Merely think, and Pisces will pick up your thoughts. Some call him perceptive; others call him psychic. Whatever term you use, you'll find this nonverbal communication baffling.

Here are a few tips that will smooth communication with Pisces:

Speak Gently

When Pisces communicates, she does it gently. You'll get better results if you do the same. Say you want to know if Pisces has sorted through the mail.

> You: Did you open the mail? Don't tell me you haven't even checked it yet.

Then you look up at Pisces, and there she isn't.

➥ *Lesson:* Forceful conversations will force Pisces to dematerialize.

Speak Clearly

Pisces can read anything into what you say. Be gentle yet clear when communicating. For example:

> You: *(to Pisces, while standing in the kitchen preparing the coq au vin)* I am making dinner.
> Pisces: *(hears)* The deconstructionist theory of literature will ultimately be judged the failure of twentieth-century literary criticism.

➥ *Lesson:* If what you're saying is important, ask Pisces to repeat it back to you so there's no confusion.

Call Pisces Anytime

You won't disturb Pisces. You won't reach her, either. You'll reach an answering machine. It's not that Pisces doesn't want to talk to you. She just wants to slip space between herself and others.

Distance is the only way she can protect herself against her own relentlessly rescuing nature and other people's demands.

Pisces uses all the communication-buffering devices: voice mail, caller-ID, unlisted telephone numbers, post office boxes. This is a problem when you want something simple: like a conversation.

↬ *Lesson:* Get comfortable leaving messages. Pisces will get in touch with you. Eventually.

The Slippery Soul Mate: The Pisces Lover

Are you into emotion? Otherworldly romance? Creative truth-telling? Then you've found the right lover in Pisces.

Pisces is the romantic spellbinder of the zodiac. Sensitive. Caring. Sensual. The Fish are always being taken for soul mates. Say you're tired of your current, stable lover. You sigh as you imagine your ideal: "I'd like someone who feels, not just thinks. Someone creative. Tuned in. An artist, maybe, with curly hair and a classic car."

Here comes Pisces. And Pisces is guess what?

A tuned-in artist with wavy hair. As for the car, who cares? It's close enough. You sent your signal out into the cosmos, and Pisces felt it karmically necessary to approach you. Or if you're more inclined to the mundane, Pisces picked up hints about what you long for in a lover. Then obligingly shape-shifted into what you wanted.

↬ *Lesson:* Pisces is tuned into more than just art. He's tuned into you and will become what you want—but only when he wants.

Of course Pisces is your soul mate. You were made for each other. You got what you asked for and a whole lot more. Consider the extras: a waif he said could crash at your place until he finds a job, stray pets of all manner, as well as a string of devoted spouses/exes of various descriptions and quality. That's the price of Pisces' compassion and sensitivity.

Pisces Turn-Ons

To Pisces, romance is more than lilies, Puccini, and candlelit dinners. It goes deeper than that, down to the depths of the relationship's soul, your past lives, and Pisces' current neuroses. Turn on Pisces by doing the following:

Act helpless. Pisces wants to rescue you. It makes her feel needed. So misplace your car keys. Get lost on your way to the grocery store. Forget how to operate a washing machine.

➳ *Lesson:* Pisces sympathizes with your ineptitude. It means she can help.

Adopt a nonjudgmental attitude. Or pretend to. Pisces doesn't make moral judgments and avoids people who do. Say you're at a luncheon where the main course is gossip about the latest arrest on Wall Street. While everyone's condemning the accused, say something like this: "Let's not be too hard on him. Maybe he had a good reason to embezzle funds and dabble in insider trading."

Share your tragic past. Remember, sympathy is the Pisces Achilles' heel. Pisces especially sympathizes with tragedy. If a tragic history is past praying for, borrow one. (For ideas, read Thomas Hardy or the whole of Russian literature.)

Feign indecisiveness. Pisces likes for people to be flexible. Let's say you have a date with Pisces and can either go to a movie or out to dinner. You'd like to try a new Italian restaurant. How should you handle the situation? Try this:

> You: I don't care if we see *Casablanca* or eat cannelloni. What do you want to do?
>
> Pisces: Oh, you choose.
>
> You: No, you choose.

Go back and forth a few times, then say: "How about dinner?"

Lesson: Act indecisive. You'll make Pisces happy and get credit for being easygoing.

Be noncommittal. Use phrases like "Oh, well" and "whatever." It sounds as though you have no unreasonable expectations, either of Pisces or the relationship. It's not that Pisces is unable to make commitments. It's just that she can't keep them.

Lesson: Commitments make Pisces nervous. Don't make them, and don't ask Pisces to, either.

Pisces Turn-Offs

Pisces may be easygoing, but there are a couple of things you shouldn't do around him.

Don't make waves. Pisces doesn't like pushy people. If you use force, the Fish will swim away.

> You: *(after an electrical short has fused the house into darkness)* Why didn't you tell me the electrician said the house needed to be rewired?

Pisces smiles, and then volunteers to help.

> Pisces: I'll go out and buy some candles.

Then Pisces spends the rest of the day choosing between scented votives or dripless tapers.

Lesson: If you scold Pisces in a confrontational way, he'll leave.

Don't hold Pisces accountable. As in, don't ask where the Fish has been, what she's been doing, and with whom she's been doing it. Of course, Pisces is anxious to please and will answer your questions even though she doesn't want to.

> You: Why didn't you come home last night?

Pisces tells you about ministering to an ailing friend, about the Siamese she rescued on the interstate, and the funeral procession that slowed her down. You finally tell her to stop, because your vision is blurred by tears and you've run out of tissues.

Later, you find out that Pisces told the truth, but not the whole truth and nothing but.

⇢ *Lesson:* Pisces lovers recognize the truth but were never encouraged to share it with other people.

How to Secretly Keep Tabs on Pisces

Pisces is indirect. The way he sees it, why go the direct route when the circuitous one affords better scenery? It also has the added bonus of making it hard for you to follow him.

So it follows that you can't ask direct questions and get direct answers. All they'll do is send Pisces around the corner to buy a pack of cigarettes, a five-minute drive that Pisces will stretch into a week to avoid your insensitivity and prying.

So you'll have to outmaneuver Pisces. Learn how to look beyond the illusion and into reality. The following table contains examples of questions you shouldn't ask Pisces, followed by actions you can take to find the answers:

QUESTION NOT TO ASK	HOW TO FIND THE ANSWER
"Did you go to work or a movie?"	Check the mileage on the car.
"Did you mail the car payment?"	Call the loan company.
"Did you make plane reservations?"	Call your travel agent.

While these may seem the acts of a private detective, law enforcement officer, or other paranoid person, they're the only way to deal with Pisces and still keep informed and sane.

Will Pisces think you're spying on him? Yes. But Pisces always suspects he's under surveillance. So what do you have to lose?

The Pisces Boss

The Pisces boss is an endangered species, and yours is one of the few left. Pisces doesn't like being a boss, never had the ambition to become one, and is now trying to work her way down the ladder.

Until she does, be gentle with her. It's the best way to get what you want. Dealing with the Pisces boss is fairly easy. The lack of emotional involvement brings out all the best and easy-to-manipulate Neptunian traits.

Taking Advantage of the Pisces Boss

A Pisces boss is very understanding and easy to please. He's generous with raises, personal leave, and vacations. He's also generous with sympathy, and everyone from upper management to clerical support knows it. You'll often find people asking for his advice, crying on his shoulder, or trying to pick his pockets. You can use Pisces sympathy to your advantage, too.

Here's how to get your way with the Pisces boss:

Play on her compassion. You're late to a meeting. Your Pisces boss merely stands outside the conference room. She doesn't say anything, because she can't bear to pin anyone down, mostly because somebody might try to pin *her* down.

You: The most horrible thing has happened.

Pisces pulls out a handkerchief, forgetting she has a boss herself—one who is not a Pisces and is waiting impatiently for both of you so they can begin the meeting.

You: *(drying your eyes after crying on her shoulder about your ailing mother, deadbeat boyfriend, and the escalating tension in the Middle East)* I feel better now. You're very understanding.

Pisces nods. She knows. Your tardiness and the roomful of now-exasperated colleagues are forgiven and practically forgotten.

Pisces: Let's go into that meeting now, shall we?

➻ *Lesson:* Slip past Pisces' reprimands by playing on Pisces' sympathy. **Give to your Pisces boss's favorite charity.** Your Pisces boss is compassionate and expects you to be the same. If you don't sign over one percent of your salary to his pet charity, Pisces will cross your name off his list of people to promote. This is the one area in which the Pisces sympathy fails.

➻ *Lesson:* If you're unsympathetic to the ill or oppressed, Pisces will forget his own compassion when your performance review comes due. **Play on Pisces' superstitions.** The superstition varies from Pisces to Pisces. But it's always there. It might be Martian spirituality, organized religion, or any opiate of the moment. Use it to your advantage.

Here's the scenario: Your Pisces boss is working up to reprimand you for taking a three-week vacation.

You: How did it happen that I got to work with you? It must've been destiny. (Or fate. Or manifesting. Or manifest destiny.)

How to Advance on the Pisces Boss

Yes, the Pisces boss is generous with raises and promotions. But the easiest way to get a raise is to resort to larceny and steal his job. Don't feel guilty. Feel happy. Pisces does. Why? Because he'd rather not be a boss. Yes, this is a strange concept, especially to more businesslike signs of the zodiac like Aries, Taurus, Gemini, Cancer, Leo, Virgo, Libra, Scorpio, Sagittarius, Capricorn, and Aquarius.

Keeping this in mind, you won't have to wait long before Pisces slips a gilt-edged thank-you note into your in-box. Then vanishes.

Pisces is quite slippery. It's hard to get a grip on the Fish. The biggest problem is Pisces' escapist tendencies. What could Pisces want to escape from? Just about anything. The best way to give the Fish a manipulative run for her money is not to try to get a grip on her. Instead, grasp gently, and you'll get a shot at getting what you want.

15

Sun Sign and Rising Sign Combinations

Maybe you've read a sun sign astrology book and the description barely fits your lover, boss, or friend. Is the sun sign description off? Or are they exceptions?

They are exceptions. Your lover, boss, or friend is that rarity: a subtle Aries, a sloppy Virgo, a together Pisces, a tactful Sagittarius, a corporately clueless Capricorn, a celibate Scorpio, a reliable Gemini, a conformist Aquarius, an erratic Taurus, a travel-addicted Cancer, a retiring Leo, or a trouble-loving Libra.

The sun sign description isn't necessarily wrong; it's just part of the astrological picture. But it's not the only part. The rising sign is also important. The traits shown by each are valid facets of anyone's personality.

Knowing a person's rising sign gives you extra leverage in dealing with them. Don't forget that the traits of the sign and the tactics to use with a particular sign are the same, whether they're the sun sign or rising sign. We can best get our way with other people by playing on both.

Reminder: See Chapter 2 for information about how to find the rising sign, and tips on how to use the sun sign and rising sign together.

If you don't find the sun sign and rising sign combination you're looking for, just reverse the order of the signs. For example, you'll find Pisces/Virgo and Virgo/Pisces.

If the sun and rising sign traits seem contradictory, be compassionate. You just have to visit the person's mind. Think what it must be like to live in it.

1. Aries/Taurus: Aries Sun Sign or Aries Rising with Taurus Sun Sign or Taurus Rising

The combination of Aries impetuosity and Taurus prudence is a clash between recklessness and deliberation. The Taurus energy yields a person who approaches things with a thoroughness that's fatiguing to watch. The Bullish side of a Ram/Bull is big on planning. This is what prompted him to make a life plan. You may wonder why it's written in crayon: That's because he made it at the age of eight. Don't expect him to deviate from it.

On the other hand, his Aries side thrives on crisis management. The Aries influence makes for a slap-dash way of doing things. Needless to say, an Aries/Taurus person is pulled between these two different ways of acting and reacting. Your Aries/Taurus friend, lover, or boss will flash one side of his nature, then the other. The result is confusion (for you).

For instance, when the Taurus side appears, he'll become careful. When faced with a course of action, he'll consider, reconsider, think about it, and then make plans. Let's say the two of you are planning to take a weekend trip. The Bull/Ram is trying to decide whether it's more economical to drive, take a train, or ride a bus. He'll look at maps, consult the bus schedules and railway timetables, call AAA, check on gas prices, and so on. Then a mere three days later, he'll decide to take a plane because it's faster.

Where did that option come from? you ask. It came from his

impetuous, impatient Aries side who'd rather die than sit in a car, train, or bus for more than an hour. His Aries and Taurus sides will pop up in random order to torment you.

Become flexible.

2. Aries/Gemini: Aries Sun Sign or Aries Rising with Gemini Sun Sign or Gemini Rising

Aries likes to do things quickly. Gemini likes to do things even more quickly. Keep in mind that Aries/Gemini is the master sprinter of the zodiac. With an Aries/Gemini, you're dealing with someone who thinks, speaks, and hears in shorthand. Anytime you communicate with Aries/Gemini, get to the point. For example, does she want to hear the latest news? Instead of relating the world news roundup, give her a synopsis of the headlines. Is she looking for entertainment? She's the person at the video store asking where she can find the sixty-minute version of *Gone with the Wind*.

For example, maybe you work for her. She has given you a multitude of tasks to do ASAP. React immediately, and make sure she sees you take action. Wait until she flits off to lunch. Then shift into a contemplative mood and sift through the stack of to-dos she's given you. There are so many, you'll be tempted to throw some of them away. Don't. Chances are the memo you'd like to send to the landfill is the one she wants you to follow up on most. For now, focus on one thing and forget about the other items on the list. With any luck, her forgetful Gemini side will prompt her to forget, too— preferably forever.

3. Aries/Cancer: Aries Sun Sign or Aries Rising with Cancer Sun Sign or Cancer Rising

This combination is a curious mixture of recklessness and conservatism. Being this way could drive the Ram/Crab crazy. Being around it could drive you even crazier, especially in a financial situation. Your

Aries/Cancer friend, lover, or boss is liable to spend lots of money and then feel guilty about it. It would be fine if he kept his financial angst to himself, but he rarely does.

Whenever you indulge in a shopping spree, he wants you to follow his example and go on a guilt trip afterward. You're not keen to do penance and, besides, you left your hair shirt at the cleaners along with Aries/Cancer's favorite dress slacks.

When he starts rifling through your receipts and then reminds you how unstable the stock market is and how hard it is to get good value for money, it's tempting to ignore him or to hide the spoils from future shopping excursions. But it's better to appease him. The best way to do this is to pretend to feel guilty.

Just say, "I'm sorry about that."

It sounds as though you're sorry you went shopping. Actually, you're sorry about the stock market and the fact that it's hard to get good value for money. So, you're not really accepting the guilt. You are, however, addressing his concerns. And that'll get you off the hook—every time.

4. Aries/Leo: Aries Sun Sign or Aries Rising with Leo Sun Sign or Leo Rising

With your domineering Aries/Leo friend, lover, or boss, you're dealing with the ultimate ego. This quality is impossible to ignore, which is a good thing because you'll be in trouble if you do. You'd like to keep Aries/Leo happy, so you continue to fork over the flattery. But sometimes when you indulge in these social niceties, you feel as if you're overdoing it. Or maybe you even feel as if you're lying. Is there a way to give Aries/Leo what she wants and keep your integrity at the same time?

Try using ambiguous statements like the following:

If Aries/Leo has been away, greet her by saying, "It wasn't the same without you."

When Aries/Leo has just accomplished something, say, "You must be very proud." Aries/Leo is always proud, but this statement implies that Aries/Leo has actually done something to be proud of.

And there's always the ever-useful statement you can trot out on occasions when Aries/Leo lectures you (which is all the time): "You have a point." Of course, you didn't say whether it was a good or a bad point. You can just keep that part to yourself.

5. Aries/Virgo: Aries Sun Sign or Aries Rising with Virgo Sun Sign or Virgo Rising

Aries likes to take the lead, and Virgo likes to take matters into his own hands when he thinks you're making a mess of things. Your Aries/Virgo friend, boss, or lover combines the gentle criticism of Virgo with the Aries tendency to take charge. Now that you've attracted an Aries/Virgo into your life, you'll rarely get the chance to do anything for yourself again.

For instance, Aries/Virgo sees you slapping a bunch of stamps onto a package in an obvious attempt to estimate how much it will cost to send a package at the new postage rates.

He says, "I'll be happy to take this package to the post office."

You smile at this thoughtfulness. As soon as he returns, he says, "It was just as I thought: You used too many stamps. Why didn't you weigh the package first? Then you wouldn't have wasted all that postage."

This is a problem. You've taken advantage of Aries/Virgo's compulsion to help and regretted it. What started out as a relationship has become a boot camp. Of course it's sensible to get a new postage scale, but you haven't gotten around to it yet.

How do you discourage Aries/Virgo from helping anymore? The best way is to keep him occupied with a hard-to-solve problem.

This will provide entertainment for Virgo, give you some privacy, and a chance to put as much postage on your mail as your heart desires.

6. Aries/Libra: Aries Sun Sign or Aries Rising with Libra Sun Sign or Libra Rising

The mixture of Aries and Libra produces friction. Libra's peacemaking persuasiveness and Aries' bossy bravado doesn't mix easily. On one hand, the Libra side of your Aries/Libra friend, lover, or boss would like for the atmosphere to be peaceful and harmonious. On the other hand, the Aries side wants the excitement of shaking things up. You may wonder why Aries/Libra breaches the peace she worked so hard to foster. Think of it this way: How else can she fulfill her Libra side's peacemaking function unless there's unease around her? Yes, it can be unnerving to go from one extreme to another, but console yourself with this fact: Whatever the atmosphere is like today, it will be different tomorrow. Guaranteed.

7. Aries/Scorpio: Aries Sun Sign or Aries Rising with Scorpio Sun Sign or Scorpio Rising

Aries/Scorpios can be very passionate. The phrase *wishy-washy* is not in his verbal arsenal. He relates life and emotion to the colors of the rainbow. Slide down the Ram/Scorpion's rainbow with all its colors from shimmering silver to magnificent magenta.

Before you get too excited about the view, there's just as much range in passionate Aries/Scorpio's emotional life, too. You'll experience and be on the receiving end of every emotion from euphoria to pathos. One view you won't see is the middle of the road. Moderation is much too dull. And a quality you won't be burdened with is neutrality. Watch out, this type of passion is contagious. In case it gets to be too much—and it will—learn to dodge Aries/Scorpio's passion, unless you want to end up getting passionately devoured.

8. Aries/Sagittarius: Aries Sun Sign or Aries Rising with Sagittarius Sun Sign or Sagittarius Rising

An Aries/Sagittarius type is full of it—fiery enthusiasm, that is. When in her company, you'll get swept up in a breezy atmosphere and an upbeat, fast pace. Aries/Sag is very involved in whatever she's doing, but only while she's doing it. Perhaps you work for the Ram/Archer and would like to impress your boss. In your zeal to be noticed, you start arriving early and staying late. Maybe you tack a few hours onto your timesheet on the weekend. After all of your industrious efforts, you expect your boss to be thrilled. For once, Aries/Sag isn't. The reason? If Aries/Sagittarius isn't in the office, the building itself doesn't exist.

It's much better to be busy (or act busy) while she's there. Grab a stack of papers and dash back and forth in front of her office. You don't actually have to be running anywhere. By just acting maniacally busy, you'll capture her attention. And maybe earn a raise.

9. Aries/Capricorn: Aries Sun Sign or Aries Rising with Capricorn Sun Sign or Capricorn Rising

When the signs of Aries and Capricorn collide, there's a fundamental difference in outlook. Aries is idealistic; Capricorn can be pessimistic. In Aries' world, there's a refreshing quality of idealism. He keeps this freshness of outlook no matter how old he is or how many disasters he's experienced. Such faith is endearing, and most people would consider it a delightful sign of faith. Others consider it a blind refusal to assimilate experience. Whatever you call it, it's hard to reconcile with Capricorn's seen-it-all cynicism.

In dealing with an Aries/Capricorn friend, lover, or boss, it wouldn't hurt to emulate Aries' bright point of view. It might give you some ballast when you flop back and forth between the two philosophical extremes.

10. Aries/Aquarius: Aries Sun Sign or Aries Rising with Aquarius Sun Sign or Aquarius Rising

Aries/Aquarius is a daredevil and a trailblazer. She does everything fast and first. Rarely does she stay in one place for long. If she has vanished from view, she's probably gone skydiving or car racing. The quickest way to hunt her down is by going out and about.

When she finally does come back, she'll probably be preoccupied with what she's done on her adventures. She's not self-centered—well, not entirely—but she can get preoccupied with her life and world. Keep that in mind when you deal with your Aries/Aquarius friend, boss, or lover.

Suppose you're telling Aries about corporate downsizing and what it could do to your ability to make payments on your sports car. That's when Aries decides to have a headache.

> You: They're downsizing the corporate finance department at work, and—
>
> Ram: *(interrupting and adjusting the ice pack perched atop her head)* Please turn down the TV. Or the radio. Oh, was that you talking? Please speak softly; the sound is killing my migraine.

What's the best way to handle Aries/Aquarius's apparent indifference to what happened to you today? There are many ways to get her to listen, but the best way is to pander to her liking for adventure. Make what was essentially a pedestrian day sound exotic by emphasizing the danger of corporate life. Danger will get Aries/Aquarius's attention every time.

11. Aries/Pisces: Aries Sun Sign or Aries Rising with Pisces Sun Sign or Pisces Rising

Aries is known for being robust and healthy. This health extends not only to his body but to his mind as well. He especially has a healthy ego. Pisces can be so modest that he's invisible. The merging of these two different energies is known in astrological circles as an Aries/Pisces combination; in psychology it's known as a split personality. The best way to handle this confusing combination is to be prepared for either side of the Aries/Pisces character to emerge.

Consider this: When his Aries side is showing, the Ram/Fish would love to connect with you. Do you have his phone number? If you don't, it's worth getting. Grab it and call; you'll be glad you did. He's delicious, dynamic, delightful. Ask anyone and they'll tell you. Or you can just wait and ask him yourself.

But when his Pisces side peeks out, you're treated to a display of modesty and meekness. While the Aries side is dominant, he's likely to get into all sorts of contests. It could be a contest over who gets to go first or who gets the best view when passing a mirror. But with Pisces, the all-important facet of his personality is his unassuming nature. Don't assume you can predict which side will pop up next.

12. Taurus/Gemini: Taurus Sun Sign or Taurus Rising with Gemini Sun Sign or Gemini Rising

When Taurus is matched with Gemini, there's a cosmic clash between the two energies. Taurus is cautious; Gem is careless. Taurus likes to plan; Gemini likes to be spontaneous. Gemini likes to circulate money; Taurus wants to hang onto it. Your Taurus/Gemini lover, friend, or boss will never be able to make up her mind whether she wants to finance the lottery or win it. The resulting financial schizophrenia of an astrological combination like this is best observed from the outside. So even though it's a pain in the ass to deal with the Bull/Twins, it's an even bigger pain to actually be one.

13. Taurus/Cancer: Taurus Sun Sign or Taurus Rising with Cancer Sun Sign or Cancer Rising

A Taurus/Cancer loves home with a passion that's immoral. He loves financial security almost as much. Some unkind people say that the Crab/Bull is tightfisted. For example, maybe he goes shopping for accessories for his home. When he gets back, he's proud of what he's bought. After you peer into his packages, you're sure you don't know why. It has apparently escaped Taurus/Cancer's notice that the candles were on sale because their wicks are missing.

14. Taurus/Leo: Taurus Sun Sign or Taurus Rising with Leo Sun Sign or Leo Rising

The pairing of Taurus and Leo emphasizes the quality of loyalty. Your Bull/Lion boss, lover, or friend is unfashionably loyal. When everyone else is job shopping and company hopping, he's savoring the promotion he's gained after ten years with the same company. When newspapers declare the divorce rate is still rising, he buys a Lalique swan as a gift to celebrate his twelfth anniversary. If this sounds too good to be true, it isn't. The bummer is that not only is Taurus/Leo loyal, but he expects you to be, too. This can be a real problem if you're fickle and deal with honor on a strictly sliding scale. With his tendency to stick with things and people for a long time, you'll have years (maybe even decades) to enjoy being the focus of his attention—his undivided, undiluted, interminable attention.

15. Taurus/Virgo: Taurus Sun Sign or Taurus Rising with Virgo Sun Sign or Virgo Rising

The Taurus/Virgo home is a warm, welcoming place. Taurus tempers the Virgo attraction to Euro-spare industrial lofts that have all the warmth of a psychiatrist's waiting room without the benefit of comforting magazines. Taurus/Virgos make homes cozy and comfortable. They have better things to do than devote themselves to straightening, restraightening, and measuring the space between the ornaments that adorn the room.

Similarly, Bull/Virgins make delightful houseguests. Anyone who says that they look at everything with a critical eye is just wrong. Taurus/Virgos are sociable creatures; they'd rather have sparkling conversations with their hosts instead of straightening their pictures, criticizing their manners, and resetting their dinner table in the proper way. Taurus/Virgo will love your home almost as much as you do. Then what's the problem? Getting her there. Virgo loves routine, and one of Taurus's routines involves staying home whenever possible. So enjoy her company in either your home or hers. Chances are, your Taurus/Virgo's social life will revolve around it.

16. Taurus/Libra: Taurus Sun Sign or Taurus Rising with Libra Sun Sign or Libra Rising

If you're having a tough day, be glad you're going home to Taurus/ Libra. Taurus is tactile; Libra is soothing. When you're cradled in this kind of comfort, not only will you forget about your bad day, you'll probably even forget you have a job.

Keep this sensation in mind when you'd like to finagle something from your Taurus/Libra lover or friend. He's sensitive to touch: If you can get your hands on him, you'll have no trouble getting your hands on just about anything else you want.

17. Taurus/Scorpio: Taurus Sun Sign or Taurus Rising with Scorpio Sun Sign or Scorpio Rising

With the fusion of Taurus with Scorpio, the result is a sensuous and stubborn individual. One way these qualities manifest themselves is in a passion for resources: sexual (Scorpio) and material (Taurus). This passion can work to your advantage, though. When the Bull doesn't want to part with money, appeal to the Scorpio side's baser instincts.

Let's say you're living with the Bull/Scorpion. You're trying to persuade her to invest in a new couch. Unfortunately, the one you like is expensive. With that in mind, the best way to talk her into buying it is to point out that quality is always more expensive. Besides, the superior construction will hold up better during your passionate lovemaking sessions on the sofa. Don't be surprised if you're in a position to test out the springs on your new couch that same evening.

18. Taurus/Sagittarius: Taurus Sun Sign or Taurus Rising with Sagittarius Sun Sign or Sagittarius Rising

Your Taurus/Sagittarius friend, boss, or lover faces a few challenges. The most important is his conflicting needs. His Taurus side needs safety, security, and predictability. His Sagittarius side craves danger and excitement. One day, Taurus/Sagittarius will be pricing moonlight hot-air balloon rides. The next day, he'll moan that if the stock market keeps fluctuating, he won't be able to afford balloons for his son's birthday party. Which mind-set reflects what's really going on? Who cares, as long as he can't get his mitts on your checkbook?

19. Taurus/Capricorn: Taurus Sun Sign or Taurus Rising with Capricorn Sun Sign or Capricorn Rising

This pairing of earthy Taurus and practical Capricorn yields an iron-clad traditionalist. If you're an avant-garde type who's into the newest fashions and the current diet craze, the Bull/Goat will remind you of the days when smoking was considered healthy and meat was one of the four food groups. This philosophy will extend to her thinking in almost everything from politics to pregnancy. Since you're unlikely to shake her convictions, keep your radical notions to yourself.

20. Taurus/Aquarius: Taurus Sun Sign or Taurus Rising with Aquarius Sun Sign or Aquarius Rising

Would you start building a new home without an architect's plan? No, and you shouldn't try to manipulate Taurus/Aquarius without one, either. Taurus/Aquarius loves plans (sometimes). He also loves to be impulsive.

With Taurus/Aquarius, saving is a craving: He likes to save money and rescue the rain forests, no matter how much it costs. He wants the stability of a secure home base and the excitement of being on the geographical move. You may sense contradictions here. Good. You'll need all of your flexibility to keep up with the mental contortions that result from combining the Bull with the Water Bearer.

21. Taurus/Pisces: Taurus Sun Sign or Taurus Rising with Pisces Sun Sign or Pisces Rising

Down-to-earth Taurus has to be able to see or touch something for it to be real. Creative Pisces just has to imagine something and it will materialize. The teaming of Taurus and Pisces can result in one of two types of folks: either a bore who lacks imagination or a visionary who has the ability to turn dreams into reality. Keep your fingers crossed and hope your Taurus/Pisces friend, boss, or lover is one of the latter.

22. Gemini/Cancer: Gemini Sun Sign or Gemini Rising with Cancer Sun Sign or Cancer Rising

Your life with Gemini/Cancer will be as multifaceted as Gem/Cancer herself. Normally, the Cancer vibration indicates someone who's so into home that she rarely leaves it. When this energy is combined with Gemini, though, the result is a person who can't seem to remember when garbage day is but manages to memorize all of

Europe's international dialing codes. Your main problem in manipulating a Gemini/Cancer lover or family member is thinking of creative ways to coax her home. One way to keep her happy is to splurge on an ultra-high-speed Internet connection. That should keep her interested, at least until it is time for her next flight.

23. Gemini/Leo: Gemini Sun Sign or Gemini Rising with Leo Sun Sign or Leo Rising

Gemini/Leo is the social butterfly *par excellence*. The combination of Gemini movement and Leo warmth creates the kind of energy that makes you excited, makes you envious, makes you tired. This energy often manifests itself in the frenetic urge to socialize. Keep this in mind, especially if your idea of a hot Friday night is making microwave popcorn and watching Turner Classic Movies.

Or, in a work situation, maybe you assume that your job is doing your job and not frittering your time away on frivolous things like betting in the office football pool or organizing birthday card signings. Your devotion to duty is sure to pay off, you think. And certainly your productivity is up. Unfortunately, so is your time in the department. To Gemini/Leo, circulating and extracurricular activities are important—at least as important as actually putting in a day's work.

24. Gemini/Virgo: Gemini Sun Sign or Gemini Rising with Virgo Sun Sign or Virgo Rising

Words, words, words. When perpetually chatting Gemini merges with verbal Virgo, the result is a walking dictionary. Communication is paramount with the Twins/Virgin. A sure way to irritate her is to withhold communication. The silent treatment will trigger a brief moment of reflection, which will soon erupt into a one-sided conversation that's characterized by Gem/Virgo posing questions and then answering them. Then the problem is persuading her to keep her reflections to herself.

25. Gemini/Libra: Gemini Sun Sign or Gemini Rising with Libra Sun Sign or Libra Rising

When Gemini is matched with Libra, the result is the ultimate euphemizer. This person is a politician and a persuader. In astrological circles, it's common knowledge that a Gemini/Libra thought up the tactic that's known as "The Advance Appreciation Act." It goes like this: You've received a letter that thanks you for supporting a particular worthy cause. You've got the check in the envelope and are licking the flap when you realize you never actually agreed to fork over the cash. You also realize you've been thanked *now* for doing something that the composer of the letter hoped to manipulate you into doing later. You've just been exposed to the Advance Appreciation Act. This is just one of Gemini/Libra's, elegantly executed ploys. (For more, see Chapters 5 and 9.) It's likely that at some time in your life, you'll be the object of a Gem/Libra friend, lover, or boss's maneuvers. And unless you're one yourself (or are really sneaky), you may be outgunned. Just sit back, enjoy the act, and hope he has lofty motives.

26. Gemini/Scorpio: Gemini Sun Sign or Gemini Rising with Scorpio Sun Sign or Scorpio Rising

When the signs of Gem and Scorpio converge, it produces a contradictory character and quirky mind-set. The formidable Scorpio memory is legendary; the Gemini intellect is phenomenal, but her memory is nonexistent. At times, your Gemini type needs lots of reminders. To jog the memory of your Twin/Scorpion at work, leave her notes. For instance, plaster sticky notes to her computer monitor. Or to really get her attention, write a message on his computer screen in lipstick.

Do you get confused around your Gemini/Scorpio friend, lover, or boss? Sometimes Gemini/Scorpio doesn't remember anything long enough to get really pissed. But at other times, her memory of your misdemeanors is so long she'll hold them against you for the rest of your life. For instance, sometimes she can't remember her mother's maiden name; other times she never lets you forget the time you screwed her over when you were both up for a promotion at work. What's the best way to deal with it? Just be prepared to be around an erratic memory bank. And think of it this way: If she recalls just half of all the things you did wrong, you're way ahead of someone who's around an astrologically purebred Scorpio.

27. Gemini/Sagittarius: Gemini Sun Sign or Gemini Rising with Sagittarius Sun Sign or Sagittarius Rising

The Gemini tendency to flit around (mentally) along with the Sag fetish for moving around (physically) means your Twin/Archer is always on the move. Even if you manage to keep Gemini/Sag's body in one place, his mind is always circulating. And whenever you're around, chances are, you'll sense it.

For instance, maybe your Twin/Archer is a lover. Let's say you're off on a romantic weekend, and you have a suspicion that your lover is distracted. You're right.

On the surface, he happily unpacks a picnic basket and tells you how thrilled he is to be there.

Underneath the surface, he's looking at you and wondering, "Will it work out? Who's my fallback if it doesn't? Do I *really* want to be tied down with this person? What if she wears weird shoes? Or cracks her knuckles? What if she doesn't know about the current state of Italian film making? And . . ."

Yes, this can be worrisome. It could be worse, though; the internal monologue could be external, and you'd actually have to listen to it. Since Gemini/Sag's mind is so active—and so is his body—forget trying to tie this person down. Instead, think of this relationship as a trip on Gemini/Sagittarius Airlines. Just buy a ticket, board the plane, order a double espresso, and enjoy the flight.

28. Gemini/Capricorn: Gemini Sun Sign or Gemini Rising with Capricorn Sun Sign or Capricorn Rising

Capricorn is one of nature's entrepreneurs. Gemini sometimes forgets the location of her office building, not to mention the fact that she has a job. These two signs together are a collision of long-term planning and short-term thinking. With Gemini, it's a waste of breath to tell her you'll be out of town for your sister's wedding next week: She doesn't think that far ahead. Capricorn does.

Capricorn strobes on hearing phrases like *long-term outlook* or *over the next few years.* . . . Phrases like *in the short term* are the best ones to use with Gem. Which one should you use with a Gemini/Capricorn boss? Just to be on the safe side, use both.

29. Gemini/Aquarius: Gemini Sun Sign or Gemini Rising with Aquarius Sun Sign or Aquarius Rising

Gemini changeability and Aquarius unpredictability make a person who can't be pinned down. Part of the problem is that he forgets things like dental appointments, dinner dates, and staff meetings. About the only thing you can count on is the fact that he forgets. To ensure Gem/Aquarius's presence at an event, spring it on him at the last moment. Even after he has accepted, be prepared for him to change his mind because he just recalled a long-standing engagement made all of ten minutes ago. The best way to deal with this is to learn to become as flexible as Gem/Aquarius is.

30. Gemini/Pisces: Gemini Sun Sign or Gemini Rising with Pisces Sun Sign or Pisces Rising

The Gemini side indicates that she is curious, verbal, and easily distracted. She was on her way to meet you for dinner when something more interesting came along and made her forget your restaurant rendezvous. Her Pisces side is sympathetic, intuitive, and nonconfrontational.

One thing you're in for with this combination is a tendency to stand you up. The Twins/Fish might stand you up for a morning tennis game, or a dinner date, or an after-work meeting. Let's say you're at the bistro. You're starving and you've waited for an hour. Finally, you realize you're dining alone and give up on her. You really like your Gemini/Pisces pal. You'd also like her to show up on time for a change.

The next time you make contact, remember her Gemini side, which means she likes to talk. Use the opportunity to lead the conversation around to your point.

> You: It's been great talking to you. It would've been fun to talk to you over dinner the other night, though. It's not that I dislike dining alone. It's just that I was starving, and it took me awhile to figure out you weren't coming.

By mentioning how hungry you were, you've jerked the sympathetic Pisces chain. Your friend's Pisces side is full of abject apologies and will prompt Gemini/Pisces to treat you to lunch. (Tip: Take her up on her offer immediately. And it wouldn't hurt to volunteer to drive.)

31. Cancer/Leo: Cancer Sun Sign or Cancer Rising with Leo Sun Sign or Leo Rising

Because Cancer loves home and Leo loves to be loved, it's a good bet that you'll be able to sweet-talk the Crab/Lion into sprucing up the homestead. You have to be careful, though, that you approach your Cancer/Leo friend or housemate the right way. To appeal to his Cancerian side, be considerate; to grab the attention of his Leo side, be complimentary.

For instance, maybe you'd like some help in hanging new photographic prints.

As Cancer/Leo sits in front of the fireplace reading the latest Sue Grafton private eye novel, smile and say, "You look great in that sweater." By then, Cancer/Leo is feeling pleased with himself. This is the time to sneak in your request: "Do you have a few minutes? I'd love to get your opinion on something."

Cancer/Leo sighs contentedly and says, "You bet."

Lead him over to the wall where you point to one of two prints. "Do you think this one will look better here than the other one?"

Let that question lead to the next one on your agenda. By the time Cancer/Leo realizes he's been tricked into helping with the redecorating, you've already persuaded him to hammer in the nails while you stand back and urge him to scoot the picture a little to the left. Even later, when Cancer/Leo realizes he's been had, he'll be so glad the house looks nice that he won't give you too hard of a time.

Now just don't try to get him to wash the car.

32. Cancer/Virgo: Cancer Sun Sign or Cancer Rising with Virgo Sun Sign or Virgo Rising

The sensitive Cancer vibration, when blended with the courteous Virgo vibe, produces a mild and perceptive individual. With the Cancerian intuition and the Virgoan unerring ability to spot the flaws in anything or anybody, nothing much will get past her. Fortunately for you, though, the Crab/Virgin is too gentle and polite to share these insights with you. Besides, it might give you an opening to share a few of your insights into her.

The blend of Cancer's indirectness and Libra's charming diplomacy can be soothing. But if you seek the unvarnished facts, these qualities can be provoking. When you want blunt feedback, Cancer/Libra is adept at sidestepping forthright answers.

Perhaps you've just been introduced to your new coworker or your future mother-in-law. Naturally, you're anxious to discover if you've made a favorable impression. Maybe you sense a lack of warmth from the new person in your life and would like to hear Cancer/Libra's opinion. You'll get reassurance but not a straight answer.

> You: Does she like me? She seems a little distant.

Cancer/Libra has quite an arsenal of ambiguity and will use phrases like "She's a bit shy," or "She takes time to warm up to people."

These observations, while reassuring, aren't exactly reliable information. If you want a straight answer, you'll have to press. Unlike Pisces, who'll cheerfully lie, Cancer/Libra will tell you the truth. And telling the truth hurts—hurts Cancer/Libra, that is. Rather than cause this suffering, get used to translating. With the Crab/Scales, you'll be doing lots of it.

34. Cancer/Scorpio: Cancer Sun Sign or Cancer Rising with Scorpio Sun Sign or Scorpio Rising

When the signs of Cancer and Scorpio mingle, the result is an intuitive and sensitive person with powerful healing abilities and an equally powerful desire to use them. There's a snag, though: The Crab/Scorpion also requires privacy to thrive. She's sensitive to others and wants to fulfill their needs. But she finds it hard to reconcile the need to nurture with her own privacy needs. Because people can easily spot her sympathetic nature, she's a magnet for souls in trouble. The problem could be with your love life or with your mortgage company's fluctuating interest rate. Or maybe you just want directions to the post office. But how does Cancer/Scorpio know that?

Her reaction is, "Here's another person who's in trouble. How can I comfort him? How can I help him? How can I elude him?"

There's good news: You can prevent her escape by making it clear that you respect her privacy. When you see that "I've-got-to-get-out-of-here" expression, try this:

> You: I understand. You absorb other people's concerns so easily, that you feel you have to escape so you can refresh yourself.
>
> Cancer/Pisces: How perceptive of you. I tend to pop out for perspective the way other people pop out for pizza.

Smile with an expression of great understanding and sympathy. The Crab/Scorpion now shows no signs of escaping. Go ahead and tell her that sob story about your variable-rate mortgage.

35. Cancer/Sagittarius: Cancer Sun Sign or Cancer Rising with Sagittarius Sun Sign or Sagittarius Rising

The Sagittarius influence makes a person speak plainly, love travel, and tend toward wanderlust. An Archer would rather be in a B&B than in his own bedroom. He may have forgotten which newspaper he has delivered to his front doorstep, but he always remembers to keep his passport up to date. Mix that with home-loving Cancer, though, and you have a person whose favorite part of a trip is the day he comes home.

To complicate matters, the Cancer side likes to avoid issues. If left on his own, your friend, boss, or lover's Cancer side would not only like to approach issues indirectly, he'd rather not approach them at all.

The result of mixing these contradictory traits is a person who is sometimes so blunt that he scalds the skin from your bones. At other times, however, he'll not only avoid an issue, he'll avoid *you* just in case you make an issue of something.

36. Cancer/Capricorn: Cancer Sun Sign or Cancer Rising with Capricorn Sun Sign or Capricorn Rising

The combination of Cancer and Capricorn emphasizes security. Home is very important. A secure and comfortable home base provides a fertile breeding ground for the Cancer sensitivity and Capricorn class-consciousness.

Let's say you're working hard, and Cancer/Capricorn complains that you rarely go shopping or have fun or take her out to eat. You're busily working hard so you can earn the cash to do these things. While her Capricorn side is well aware of the need to work hard, her Cancerian desire for culinary cosseting overrules her restraint.

The best way to deal with this is to appeal to her security issues and penchant for living in a nice neighborhood. If she keeps interrupting work with appeals to go to the pricey French restaurant downtown, just say, "I'll be happy to stop what I'm doing so we can go out and about. While we're gone, maybe you can help me pick out which trailer park you'd like us to live in."

Cancer/Capricorn's requests will stop. Immediately.

37. Cancer/Aquarius: Cancer Sun Sign or Cancer Rising with Aquarius Sun Sign or Aquarius Rising

When the cosmos matches home-loving Cancer with radical Aquarius, the resulting personality is liable to be a domestic eccentric. One side of your Cancer/Aquarius friend, lover, or boss can't wait to stock the pantry with delectable edibles; the other side doesn't even know where the pantry is. These contradictory sides will seldom mesh, but you can encourage them to coexist by easing the domestic routine with the use of up-to-date appliances and unusual menus. Cancer/Aquarius is imbued with the microwave mentality, so stay away from dishes that take a long time to prepare. Better yet, find an exotic restaurant that delivers. That way, both sides of your Crab/Water Bearer will be happy.

38. Cancer/Pisces: Cancer Sun Sign or Cancer Rising with Pisces Sun Sign or Pisces Rising

Mysterious and secretive Crab/Scorpions are elusive but can often be found watering the lawn, tending the garden, or beating around the bush. They're supersensitive, intuitive thinkers and communicators. They can be very pleasant company; the problem is you don't know where you stand. On eggshells, probably.

Communicate carefully. Cancer/Scorpios have an uncanny ability to pick up on your thoughts—dolphins have nothing on them for radar. This nonverbal communication can be lovely, because they often do things without being asked.

For instance, maybe you get home after a hard evening's commute from work and would like nothing more than sinking into a hot bath. Before you have a chance to kick off your shoes, you hear water running and smell the soothing aroma of lavender bath salts. Remember this thoughtfulness; it'll be a comfort when you experience the downside of all this empathy and intuition.

The problem is, not only will Cancer/Scorpio read between the lines, but she's apt to see lines that aren't even there. The next time she jumps to conclusions and then jumps on your case about how insensitive you've been, just smile and recall her usual thoughtfulness. After all, it's a small price to pay.

39. Leo/Virgo: Leo Sun Sign or Leo Rising with Virgo Sun Sign or Virgo Rising

The union of Leo with Virgo yields an individual who likes to be an authority and whose mission it is to assist folks. His favorite way to help is to share his considerable knowledge. If you'd like to get your way with a Leo/Virgo friend, lover, or boss, just play on the Leo side's pride and the Virgo side's lust to help. He assumes he has a license to lecture any time, so encourage it. A time-honored ploy for getting what you want is to give him the pleasure of telling you something you already know. Maybe the Lion/Virgin launches on a lecture about the chemical composition of water. It gives him such obvious joy to tell you about H_2O that as you listen, you secretly wonder if he can't read the letters *MIT* on the diploma hanging on your wall. Just keep smiling and don't disillusion him. To compensate for the tedium of this chemistry lesson, think of all the favors he'll be in the mood to do for you now.

40. Leo/Libra: Leo Sun Sign or Leo Rising with Libra Sun Sign or Libra Rising

A Leo/Libra is mind meltingly romantic. She's endlessly considerate with everyone but especially with her *amour*. Your Leo/Libra lover will romance you with refinement. Life can be so undeniably pleasant with her, it seems a shame to spoil the atmosphere with anything so underhanded as manipulation, but here's how to do just that.

Leo/Libra has planned a picturesque vacation for the two of you in the British Virgin Islands. You'd rather go on a sporting holiday than vegetate on a beach somewhere, but how can you get your way? Try this.

You: I can't imagine anything dreamier than rubbing suntan oil all over each other on vacation this spring. But I'm really concerned about the deadly effects of skin cancer.

As Leo/Libra gasps in concern, plop down a brochure for a golfing vacation in Scotland and move in for the kill: "Wouldn't you like to jet over to Scotland? The sea breezes would be so much better for our complexions." Then smile prettily and brush up on your Gaelic.

41. Leo/Scorpio: Leo Sun Sign or Leo Rising with Scorpio Sun Sign or Scorpio Rising

Leo and Scorpio are both powerful signs and like to exercise that power by taking charge of the things (and people) around them. In the drama of life with the Lion/Scorpion, keep in mind that the Leo influence gives him charisma, and the Scorpio influence bestows magnetism. Whichever way you look at it, he's the star and that means he's in charge. You're not—or at least you should pretend you're not. If you openly challenge his position, he'll charge you with treachery and then demote you to understudy. To discourage upstarts, Leo/Scorpio has at his disposal many cosmically given weapons. Warmth and magnetism are part of his artillery, and he uses them remorselessly. His spine-chilling ability to warm you with his presence will throw you if you try to usurp his position. It's better to deal with him from a distance. Then you won't be as vulnerable.

42. Leo/Sagittarius: Leo Sun Sign or Leo Rising with Sagittarius Sun Sign or Sagittarius Rising

The warmth and enthusiasm of a Leo/Sagittarius are palpable. They are also nearly impossible to subdue. Because her psychological thermostat is controlled from the inside, you can't adjust it—you can only adjust to it. It's easy to get caught up in this kind of zeal. Your Leo/Sagittarius friend, lover, or boss can go overboard with her eagerness. One area that's particularly vulnerable is finance. In the Lion/Archer's world, budgets are boring and prudence is perverse. Keep out of her way when she goes on a spree (also keep your wallet out of reach). And when it comes to economizing, make Leo/Sagittarius happy—don't.

43. Leo/Capricorn: Leo Sun Sign or Leo Rising with Capricorn Sun Sign or Capricorn Rising

This combination can be tricky—while the Leo side embraces ostentation, the Capricorn side thinks an overt display of *anything* is vulgar. However, one thing they both crave is status. Would you like to please your Leo/Capricorn friend, lover, or boss? Acknowledge his status by giving gifts—tasteful gifts, of course, preferably in Cartier boxes. Being the recipient of this kind of respect and affection appeals to his pride and ego, of which he has more than his fair share. In fact, he has more than anyone's fair share.

Leo always displays eye-catching elegance and Capricorn likes to dress up, but you're in for a dressing-down if you treat him with anything less than the deference he deserves. You can dilute the royal displeasure by saying, "I've been meaning to ask your advice."

This tactic works because the Capricorn side likes to be considered an authority, and Leo likes being deferred to. So go ahead and ask for Leo/Capricorn's advice—you don't actually have to take it.

44. Leo/Aquarius: Leo Sun Sign or Leo Rising with Aquarius Sun Sign or Aquarius Rising

You're in for an entertainment treat with Leo/Aquarius. Imagine that life is a circus. There, in the center ring, is Leo. If Leo is the star of the show, then nonconformist Aquarius is the star of the sideshow. The more reserved astrological signs think Leo/Aquarius is flamboyant. You think she's outrageously eccentric. Sometimes her behavior gets too outrageous, and you'd like to just close your eyes and pretend she's not happening.

This isn't always possible, especially if you're in a work situation.

Remember that her Aquarius side wants to be different from everyone else, and her Leo side wants to be *better* than everyone else. Like Aries, Leo/Aquarius is an idea person. Unlike Aries, she follows up on her ideas. The Lion/Water Bearer will twirl off a few notions for you to take note of. Don't follow up on all of them; once she takes hold of a concept, she won't release it. Your Leo/Aquarius boss has a few good ideas and more than a few daft ones. Do you really want to work on a way to transmit breakfast food over the Internet? Or explore a marketing idea for dehydrated wine?

Be crafty when you want to discourage her.

As she scans the list of brainwaves, say, "That's a daring idea about the wine. I hear that one of France's favorite sports is cabernet roulette."

The Leo/Aquarius boss leans toward you with an eager expression. Before she gets too eager, say, "But I heard that somebody in France is already selling a dehydrated vintage of very, very dry cabernet."

Since Leo/Aquarius can't win with that innovative idea, you're off the hook. This time, anyway.

45. Leo/Pisces: Leo Sun Sign or Leo Rising with Pisces Sun Sign or Pisces Rising

If the marriage between the signs of Leo and Pisces were a fairy tale, it would be called "The Monarch and the Mouse." This isn't to say that the Pisces personality is in any way rodent-like, but compared to Leo it lacks authority. One thing it emphasizes in both signs is generosity and the desire to help the underdog.

Any Leo/Pisces can be outwardly imperious, but you'll be treated to that charming trait a lot if Leo/Pisces is your boss. You'll probably be told exactly what to do and what time to do it, which wash room to go to, how long you're allowed to be away from your desk, and how many sheets of toilet tissue to use.

That kind of interference will really have you reaching for your resume or the Web address of the hottest headhunting firm. Reach for a thank-you note instead. Say thanks to Leo/Pisces for giving you two weeks off to cope with your father's funeral when most bosses would've given you one. It also wouldn't hurt to express your gratitude to Leo/Pisces for treating you and your spouse to that hellacious party on your anniversary.

46. Virgo/Libra: Virgo Sun Sign or Virgo Rising with Libra Sun Sign or Libra Rising

There's an untrue astrological rumor about Virgo: that he's a fault-finding nitpicker who's impossible to live with unless you're perfect. This rumor is not only untrue, it's unfair. It's even less likely to be true when Virgo has meshed with Libra, the sign of gracious manners. Above all, Virgo/Libra yearns for order and harmony. He loves to do favors, so take advantage of it.

What might a Virgo/Libra want to do for you? He wants to make you comfortable. If the noise of a dripping faucet keeps you awake at night, he'll be happy to investigate. He won't even complain if it turns into a plumbing project that ruins his pajamas and tomorrow's big day at work. True, you'll rarely have the fun of manipulating him. But you will get out of doing all those home projects on weekends. That's not so bad, is it?

47. Virgo/Scorpio: Virgo Sun Sign or Virgo Rising with Scorpio Sun Sign or Scorpio Rising

Your mentally sharp and powerfully perceptive Virgo/Scorpio friend, lover, or boss is Sherlock Holmes, Miss Jane Marple, and Ellery Queen all rolled into one. Because of her natural detective ability, you won't be able to pull one over on her, unfortunately. If you do something she objects to, just turn yourself in, plead guilty, and hope for early parole.

48. Virgo/Sagittarius: Virgo Sun Sign or Virgo Rising with Sagittarius Sun Sign or Sagittarius Rising

The Virgo vibe endows Virgo/Sag with the ability to see all visible flaws in your world and a few of the invisible ones, too. Unfortunately, the Sag influence gives him the frankness to tell you about it—in detail, over and over. Is there a way to dodge this clarity of vision? Not really. Maybe you should just correct the problem; it's easier in the long run.

49. Virgo/Capricorn: Virgo Sun Sign or Virgo Rising with Capricorn Sun Sign or Capricorn Rising

It's sometimes said that Virgo/Capricorns are guilty of spiritual and fiscal narrow-mindedness. This is unkind as well as untrue. They have respect for all denominations, especially twenties and fifties. But sometimes they can be guilty of overly cautious behavior in the realm of romance. Maybe your love life with Virgo/Capricorn is getting routine and you'd like to try something spicier. Introduce her to the concept of wild lovemaking in safe steps. Instead of walking into the bedroom dangling a pair of handcuffs, gradually introduce her to other activities. Maybe you can pay compliments. Turn to a Victoria's Secret ad in *Vanity Fair* and say, "You'd look terrific in this little black lace number." Or one night when you're tending to dental hygiene, say, "Hey, I have a great idea for a new way to use an electric toothbrush." By taking small and safe steps, you'll soon talk Virgo/Capricorn into installing a trapeze in the bedroom—as long as it doesn't cost too much.

50. Virgo/Aquarius: Virgo Sun Sign or Virgo Rising with Aquarius Sun Sign or Aquarius Rising

Aquarius is known as one of the zodiac's greatest truth-tellers, and Virgo sees the truth with merciless clarity. With Virgo/Aquarius, it's a point of honor to see things the way they are and tell it as it is. This means you'll hear the truth from your Virgin/Water Bearer friends, bosses, or lovers whether you want to hear it or not. If you'd rather hear honeyed words instead of getting a scaldingly honest appraisal, then you're out of luck with Virgo/Aquarius. Honest.

51. Virgo/Pisces: Virgo Sun Sign or Virgo Rising with Pisces Sun Sign or Pisces Rising

The collision of Virgo rationalism with Pisces intuition can be as confusing to the person who has to deal with it as it is to the Virgin/Fish herself. Pisces tends toward casual creativity, while Virgo embraces reasoning and order. Trying to manipulate her by using logic will work sometimes; at other times you'll have to rely on intuition. The problem is you'll never know which strategy to use. It's not always possible to manipulate her by scrubbing her Revereware, cataloging her receipts, or alphabetizing her DVD collection. But if you do, you'll at least get her attention.

52. Libra/Scorpio: Libra Sun Sign or Libra Rising with Scorpio Sun Sign or Scorpio Rising

As a master manipulator and powerful persuader, Libra/Scorpio has a subtlety that makes it hard for you to detect his maneuvers. His ways and means of getting what he wants from life (and you) are too numerous to mention here (see Chapters 9 and 10 for more information). Once the Libra/Scorpio in your life has decided to plot and plan and have his wicked way with you, unfortunately there isn't much you can do about it.

53. Libra/Sagittarius: Libra Sun Sign or Libra Rising with Sagittarius Sun Sign or Sagittarius Rising

Libra and Sagittarius are two of the most loved signs of the zodiac. Cooperative, companionable Libra and straightforward, optimistic

Sagittarius are two signs that seem to be compatible with each other. When they're combined in the same person, though, there's a snag: Libra is ultra-tactful and Sagittarius is supremely tactless. Because of Libra's intuitive gifts, Libra/Sagittarius is likely to be right on target when making a careless remark. After being on the receiving end of one of those provoking comments from your Libra/Sagittarius companion, you may feel like killing her. Don't. You're sure to get convicted because of Libra/Sag's popularity. Besides, Department of Corrections orange is so unflattering to your skin tones.

54. Libra/Capricorn: Libra Sun Sign or Libra Rising with Capricorn Sun Sign or Capricorn Rising

Libra is a sign of elegance, both in appearance and manner. Libra types appreciate it if you display good manners and make kind gestures. Capricorn is refined, too, and likes the niceties of etiquette. You'll notice these traits are emphasized in a Libra/Capricorn lover, friend, or boss. Just remember that Libra/Capricorn bosses also like to follow a certain protocol. One of these traditions is the corporate chain of command. You're directly accountable to your Libra/Capricorn boss. Unlike Aries—who may be four floors above you but doesn't want to go through intermediaries or waste time riding elevators when she can use a telephone instead—Libra/Capricorn likes nods of respect.

Suppose you have a question for him. To demonstrate that you respect his time, try asking him this the next time you run into him in the hallway: "I've something I'd like to talk to you about. Should I make an appointment?" Libra/Capricorn will smile graciously and say, "How considerate of you, but that's not necessary. Let's chat about it now." He may not take you up on your offer, but he'll remember your tact and good manners. And with luck, he'll remember it the next time he writes performance reviews.

55. Libra/Aquarius: Libra Sun Sign or Libra Rising with Aquarius Sun Sign or Aquarius Rising

Sometimes Libra's obvious physical refinement disguises a highly developed intellect. When this quality is mixed with eccentrically brilliant Aquarius, the result is a highly inventive thinker. Libra/Aquarius would like for the world to be a better, more agreeable place. For example, if she's into inventions, her latest patent is for a humane form of pest control called not trapping the mouse but helping the mouse to disincarnate. After all, don't they say if you build a better mousetrap . . . ?

56. Libra/Pisces: Libra Sun Sign or Libra Rising with Pisces Sun Sign or Pisces Rising

A Libra/Pisces is smooth and soothing, ultra charming, considerate—and considerably indecisive. Harmony is an essential element of his character. Because he's nonconfrontational, making scenes is frowned upon. You certainly can't expect tantrums from him.

Maybe you're at a restaurant with your Libra/Pisces friend, lover, or boss. He engages the waiter in polite conversation, then orders eggs benedict with hollandaise sauce on the side. This means he doesn't eat hollandaise—and won't—but doesn't want to make a fuss.

Fortunately, this also means he won't make a fuss about your shortcomings—as long as you don't make a scene.

57. Scorpio/Sagittarius: Scorpio Sun Sign or Scorpio Rising with Sagittarius Sun Sign or Sagittarius Rising

In astrological circles, Sagittarius is known as a philosophical, even religious sign. For all her sexy reputation, Scorpio, too, is considered spiritual. Surely it follows, then, that your Scorpio/Sagittarius friend or lover is especially religious. It depends on your idea of religion.

Why has the monastery-myth grown like abbey walls around two of the most notoriously sexually abandoned signs of the zodiac? Imagine you're the abbot. You're pleased with Scorpio Monk. He loves the privacy but is maneuvering you into allowing him (secret) conjugal visits. In despair, you turn to Sagittarius Monk. He dropped by the abbey on his way to preach to sinners at a nearby casino, where he'll cater to a long line of sexually frustrated penitents.

58. Scorpio/Capricorn: Scorpio Sun Sign or Scorpio Rising with Capricorn Sun Sign or Capricorn Rising

Scorpio/Capricorn is quite a manipulator. He stays fairly quiet when planning his mischief. If he seems happy, carefree, and unconcerned about the future, watch out. That means he's about to pull a fast one. If you try to outmanipulate him, you could be in for a bloody battle. And while you can't count on him to act from the loftiest of motives, he's not always a Machiavellian manipulator, either. At least you can hope he's not this time.

59. Scorpio/Aquarius: Scorpio Sun Sign or Scorpio Rising with Aquarius Sun Sign or Aquarius Rising

The Scorpio essence indicates a person with incredible focus and the need to conceal what she's up to. Aquarius seems to lack focus. Some people even accuse her of being flighty. The Water Bearer circulates just about anywhere, though she's not crazy about hobnobbing with authority figures. She'd prefer that her only contact with authority is when she protests with sit-ins and drop-outs. Aquarius is not shy about expounding on her deeply felt political, social, and ethical concerns. For all of her apparently free-flowing personality, it may surprise you to find that Aquarius is just as inflexible as Scorpio. When you mix the two, you have a person who seems to be breezy and isn't.

You may think it's bad that Scorpio/Aquarius is phenomenally stubborn. Actually it's one of Scorpio/Aquarius's good points: It means she's constant. There are things she's inflexible about and always will be. Find out what they are. It varies from one Scorpio/Aquarius to another, but whatever it is it's non-negotiable. Maybe she goes to the library the same day each week, or mails the bills from a particular post office, or gets her morning coffee at the same café every day. Be as focused as she is, and focus your efforts on working around her inflexibilities—or learning to live with them. You might as well; you have no choice.

60. Scorpio/Pisces: Scorpio Sun Sign or Scorpio Rising with Pisces Sun Sign or Pisces Rising

Intense Scorpio craves privacy, and Pisces likes to remain anonymous. When you put these two signs together, you've got an intensely private person. This doesn't mean he's unsociable or hard to get to know. He's just hard to get hold of. Maybe you'd like to establish a closer relationship with your Scorpio/Pisces acquaintance. You try the direct approach.

> You: Let's get together for a movie sometime. What's your phone number?
>
> Scorpio/Pisces: I'm uncomfortable with giving out my phone number to people I don't know very well.
>
> You: *(to yourself)* How the hell do you expect to get to know people well if you don't talk to them first?
>
> You: *(to Scorpio/Pisces)* Well, is your number in the phone book?
>
> Scorpio/Pisces: Not exactly. But my name's in the phone book.

As you may gather, this conversation is getting nowhere. It looks like the acquaintanceship will go nowhere, too. And if you try to force information from him, he'll be forced to tell an untruth. (That's what you'd get for being pushy.)

Try this: Give the Scorpion/Fish your phone number, then maybe he'll reciprocate. Even if he doesn't share his phone number with you, chances are he'll take the initiative and call you. Eventually.

61. Sagittarius/Capricorn: Sagittarius Sun Sign or Sagittarius Rising with Capricorn Sun Sign or Capricorn Rising

Sagittarius is undeniably delightful company. It's fortunate that Sag is good at being gregarious because the other thing she's good at—being tactless—can be a real problem. This quality of dropping conversational bricks is embarrassing to most of the other signs, but Capricorn finds it especially mortifying. When Sagittarius is combined with Capricorn, the result is a person whose attempts to smooth over conversational gaffes are as smooth as sandpaper. Your Sagittarius/Capricorn friend, lover, or boss deserves understanding and, above all, forgiveness for getting caught in the occasional social snafu. After all, someone should forgive her—her Capricorn side never will.

62. Sagittarius/Aquarius: Sagittarius Sun Sign or Sagittarius Rising with Aquarius Sun Sign or Aquarius Rising

Honesty is one of the hallmarks of both Sagittarius and Aquarius. Independence is another. When the two signs mesh, though, the need for independence sometimes overrides the penchant for honesty.

The closer Sagittarius/Aquarius gets geographically and intellectually, the more unavailable he becomes emotionally. While this usually isn't a problem if it's a professional association, a love relationship—specifically, a committed love relationship—can be trickier.

As soon as you mention the *C* word, the Archer/Water Bearer gets skittish, and you can't help but notice the change. What happened to all that straightforwardness and directness? They're at home next to his wallet. Suddenly Sag/Aquarius can outsneak a Pisces, out-euphemize a Gemini, and outlay a Scorpio.

What can be done? A couple of coping mechanisms come to mind: You can either back off and give him more breathing room, or rethink your definition of a close relationship.

63. Sagittarius/Pisces: Sagittarius Sun Sign or Sagittarius Rising with Pisces Sun Sign or Pisces Rising

It is said that both Sagittarians and Pisceans are flimsy on follow-through. This is untrue, although one of Sagittarius/Pisces' favorite phrases is *Later*. You can take this to mean "goodbye" or as a true statement of when she intends to do whatever it is you're asking about. Lack of follow-through will seldom be a problem in her love life. Your open-minded Sagittarius/Pisces lover is a great believer in universal love, a love that embraces all creatures. This is one reason she's likely to have been intimate with everyone you know and most of the people you've never heard of. Chances are, your mind doesn't work that way. You were hoping she'd close her mind a little more just to please you. Don't worry, you'll get used to it—later.

64. Capricorn/Aquarius: Capricorn Sun Sign or Capricorn Rising with Aquarius Sun Sign or Aquarius Rising

Capricorn is a careful conservative, and Aquarius is a daring radical. There's no one like a Capricorn for preserving the status quo, and nobody like an Aquarius for smashing dogma. You can see the problem when Capricorn is combined with Aquarius. Keep it in mind at all times, because life with a Goat/Water Bearer is confusing. You'll never know which side of the political fence he'll be on. One day he'll support the death penalty; the next he'll sign a petition to ask the governor to pardon all death row inmates. This is just one example of Capricorn/Aquarius's political inconsistency, and no doubt you'll be in a position to witness many more.

65. Capricorn/Pisces: Capricorn Sun Sign or Capricorn Rising with Pisces Sun Sign or Pisces Rising

Capricorn is usually very practical and grounded in her thinking. Pisces' fanciful thinking often takes her mind to remote places, like the outer rings of Saturn. You may sense a clash here. How can you reconcile Capricorn/Pisces' two very different ways of relating to the world? It is possible. Merely tell her that you're sure you shared her belief in reincarnation in a previous life, but unfortunately you don't in this one.

66. Aquarius/Pisces: Aquarius Sun Sign or Aquarius Rising with Pisces Sun Sign or Pisces Rising

An Aquarius/Pisces is a consummate New Ager and very easy to spot. How can you miss him? He's so enlightened. He's patented so many useless inventions. After running into the Water Bearer/Fish, you decide you must be in California and wonder why you can't remember the plane ride. This person's mind, body, and spirit like to be unencumbered with worldly concerns and responsibilities. An Aquarius/Pisces friend or lover is a fairly straightforward proposition. A boss is a different story.

It's not that he's hard to get along with. It's that he'd rather not be a boss. Being an executive means sitting behind a desk in a high-rise office building, and he dislikes confinement. It means wearing a necktie; and to him, neckties are merely designer nooses. Another potential problem is that he's often late, so he feels funny about asking you to be punctual. The most serious problem is that he dislikes authority.

He seems so unhappy, and you'd like to make him feel better. Maybe he'd be happier working for a new boss. How about you?